\

HTML-5

hypertext markup language

by Zahid Wadiwale

About the Tutorial

HTML5 is the latest and most enhanced version of HTML. Technically, HTML is not a programming language, but rather a markup language. In this tutorial, we will discuss the features of HTML5 and how to use it in practice.

Audience

This tutorial has been designed for beginners in *HTML5* to make them understand the basic-to-advanced concepts of the subject.

Prerequisites

Before starting this tutorial, you should have a basic understanding of HTML and its tags.

Table of Contents

1. HTML5 – Overview

HTML5 is the next major revision of the HTML standard superseding HTML 4.01, XHTML 1.0, and XHTML 1.1. HTML5 is a standard for structuring and presenting content on the World Wide Web.

HTML5 is a cooperation between the World Wide Web Consortium (W3C) and the Web Hypertext Application Technology Working Group (WHATWG).

The new standard incorporates features like video playback and drag-and-drop that have been previously dependent on third-party browser plug-ins such as Adobe Flash, Microsoft Silverlight, and Google Gears.

Browser Support

The latest versions of Apple Safari, Google Chrome, Mozilla Firefox, and Opera all support many HTML5 features and Internet Explorer 9.0 will also have support for some HTML5 functionality.

The mobile web browsers that come pre-installed on iPhones, iPads, and Android phones all have excellent support for HTML5.

New Features

HTML5 introduces a number of new elements and attributes that can help you in building modern websites. Here is a set of some of the most prominent features introduced in HTML5.

- **New Semantic Elements:** These are like <header>, <footer>, and <section>.

- **Forms 2.0:** Improvements to HTML web forms where new attributes have been introduced for <input> tag.

- **Persistent Local Storage:** To achieve without resorting to third-party plugins.

- **WebSocket :** A next-generation bidirectional communication technology for web applications.

- **Server-Sent Events:** HTML5 introduces events which flow from web server to the web browsers and they are called Server-Sent Events (SSE).

- **Canvas:** This supports a two-dimensional drawing surface that you can program with JavaScript.

- **Audio & Video:** You can embed audio or video on your webpages without resorting to third-party plugins.

- **Geolocation:** Now visitors can choose to share their physical location with your web application.

- **Microdata:** This lets you create your own vocabularies beyond HTML5 and extend your web pages with custom semantics.

- **Drag and drop:** Drag and drop the items from one location to another location on the same webpage.

Backward Compatibility

HTML5 is designed, as much as possible, to be backward compatible with existing web browsers. Its new features have been built on existing features and allow you to provide fallback content for older browsers.

It is suggested to detect support for individual HTML5 features using a few lines of JavaScript.

2. HTML5 – Syntax

The HTML 5 language has a "custom" HTML syntax that is compatible with HTML 4 and XHTML1 documents published on the Web, but is not compatible with the more esoteric SGML features of HTML 4.

HTML 5 does not have the same syntax rules as XHTML where we needed lower case tag names, quoting our attributes, an attribute had to have a value and to close all empty elements.

HTML5 comes with a lot of flexibility and it supports the following features –

- Uppercase tag names.

- Quotes are optional for attributes.

- Attribute values are optional.

- Closing empty elements are optional.

The DOCTYPE

DOCTYPEs in older versions of HTML were longer because the HTML language was SGML based and therefore required a reference to a DTD.

HTML 5 authors would use simple syntax to specify DOCTYPE as follows:

```
<!DOCTYPE html>
```

The above syntax is case-insensitive.

Character Encoding

HTML 5 authors can use simple syntax to specify Character Encoding as follows –

```
<meta charset="UTF-8">
```

The above syntax is case-insensitive.

The <script> tag

It's common practice to add a type attribute with a value of "text/javascript" to script elements as follows –

```
<script type="text/javascript" src="scriptfile.js"></script>
```

HTML 5 removes extra information required and you can use simply following syntax –

```
<script src="scriptfile.js"></script>
```

The \<link\> tag

So far you were writing \<link\> as follows −

```
<link rel="stylesheet" type="text/css" href="stylefile.css">
```

HTML 5 removes extra information required and you can simply use the following syntax −

```
<link rel="stylesheet" href="stylefile.css">
```

HTML5 Elements

HTML5 elements are marked up using start tags and end tags. Tags are delimited using angle brackets with the tag name in between.

The difference between start tags and end tags is that the latter includes a slash before the tag name.

Following is the example of an HTML5 element −

```
<p>...</p>
```

HTML5 tag names are case insensitive and may be written in all uppercase or mixed case, although the most common convention is to stick with lowercase.

Most of the elements contain some content like \<p\>...\</p\> contains a paragraph. Some elements, however, are forbidden from containing any content at all and these are known as void elements. For example, **br**, **hr**, **link**, **meta**, etc.

HTML5 Attributes

Elements may contain attributes that are used to set various properties of an element.

Some attributes are defined globally and can be used on any element, while others are defined for specific elements only. All attributes have a name and a value and look like as shown below in the example.

Following is the example of an HTML5 attribute which illustrates how to mark up a **div** element with an attribute named class using a value of "example" −

```
<div class="example">...</div>
```

Attributes may only be specified within start tags and must never be used in end tags.

HTML5 attributes are case insensitive and may be written in all uppercase or mixed case, although the most common convention is to stick with lowercase.

HTML5 Document

The following tags have been introduced for better structure –

- **section:** This tag represents a generic document or application section. It can be used together with h1-h6 to indicate the document structure.

- **article:** This tag represents an independent piece of content of a document, such as a blog entry or newspaper article.

- **aside:** This tag represents a piece of content that is only slightly related to the rest of the page.

- **header:** This tag represents the header of a section.

- **footer:** This tag represents a footer for a section and can contain information about the author, copyright information, et cetera.

- **nav:** This tag represents a section of the document intended for navigation.

- **dialog:** This tag can be used to mark up a conversation.

- **figure:** This tag can be used to associate a caption together with some embedded content, such as a graphic or video.

The markup for an HTML 5 document would look like the following –

```
<!DOCTYPE html>
<html>

   <head>
      <meta charset="utf-8">
      <title>...</title>
   </head>

   <body>
      <header>...</header>
      <nav>...</nav>

      <article>
         <section>

            ...
         </section>
      </article>
```

```
      <aside>...</aside>
      <footer>...</footer>
   </body>
</html>
```

```
<!DOCTYPE html>

<html>

   <head>
      <meta charset="utf-8">
      <title>...</title>
   </head>

   <body>

      <header role="banner">
         <h1>HTML5 Document Structure Example</h1>
         <p>This page should be tried in safari, chrome or Mozila.</p>
      </header>

      <nav>


         <ul>
            <li><a href="http://www.w3schools.com/html">HTML
Tutorial</a></li>
               <li><a  href="http://www.w3schools.com/css">CSS
 Tutorial</a></li>
         <li><a href="http://www.w3schools.com/javascript">JavaScript
Tutorial</a></li>
         </ul>

      </nav>

      <article>
         <section>
            <p>Once article can have multiple sections</p>
```

```
                </section>
        </article>


        <aside>
            <p>This is  aside part of the web page</p>
        </aside>


        <footer>
            <p>Created by <a
href="http://zahidserver.runhosting.net/">Zahid  Wadiwale</a></p>
</footer>
        </body> </html>
```

It will produce the following result –

HTML5 Document Structure Example

This page should be tried in safari, chrome or Mozila.

- HTML Tutorial
- CSS Tutorial
- JavaScript Tutorial

Once article can have multiple sections

This is aside part of the web page

Created by zahid wadiwale

3. HTML5 – Attributes

As explained in the previous chapter, elements may contain attributes that are used to set various properties of an element.

Some attributes are defined globally and can be used on any element, while others are defined for specific elements only. All attributes have a name and a value and look like as shown below in the example.

Following is the example of an HTML5 attributes which illustrates how to mark up a div element with an attribute named class using a value of "example" −

```
<div class="example">...</div>
```

Attributes may only be specified within **start tags** and must never be used in **end tags**.

HTML5 attributes are case insensitive and may be written in all uppercase or mixed case, although the most common convention is to stick with lowercase.

Standard Attributes

The attributes listed below are supported by almost all the HTML 5 tags.

Attribute	Options	Function
accesskey	User Defined	Specifies a keyboard shortcut to access an element.
align	right, left, center	Horizontally aligns tags
background	URL	Places an background image behind an element
bgcolor	numeric, hexidecimal, RGB values	Places a background color behind an element
class	User Defined	Classifies an element for use with Cascading Style Sheets.
contenteditable	true, false	Specifies if the user can edit the element's content or not.
contextmenu	Menu id	Specifies the context menu for an element.
data-XXXX	User Defined	Custom attributes. Authors of a HTML document can define their own attributes. Must start with "data-".
draggable	true,false, auto	Specifies whether or not a user is allowed to drag an element.

height	Numeric Value	Specifies the height of tables, images, or table cells.
hidden	hidden	Specifies whether element should be visible or not.
id	User Defined	Names an element for use with Cascading Style Sheets.
item	List of elements	Used to group elements.
itemprop	List of items	Used to group items.
spellcheck	true, false	Specifies if the element must have it's spelling or grammar checked.
style	CSS Style sheet	Specifies an inline style for an element.
subject	User define id	Specifies the element's corresponding item.
tabindex	Tab number	Specifies the tab order of an element.
title	User Defined	"Pop-up" title for your elements.
valign	top, middle, bottom	Vertically aligns tags within an HTML element.
width	Numeric Value	Specifies the width of tables, images, or table cells.

For a complete list of HTML5 Tags and related attributes, please check our reference to HTML5 Tags.

Custom Attributes

A new feature being introduced in HTML 5 is the addition of custom data attributes.

A custom data attribute starts with **data-** and would be named based on your requirement. Here is a simple example −

```
<div class="example" data-subject="physics" data-level="complex">
   ...
</div>
```

The above code will be perfectly valid HTML5 with two custom attributes called *data-subject* and *data-level*. You would be able to get the values of these attributes using JavaScript APIs or CSS in similar way as you get for standard attributes.

4. HTML5 – Events

When users visit your website, they perform various activities such as clicking on text and images and links, hover over defined elements, etc. These are examples of what JavaScript calls **events**.

We can write our event handlers in Javascript or VBscript and you can specify these event handlers as a value of event tag attribute. The HTML5 specification defines various event attributes as listed below –

We can use the following set of attributes to trigger any **javascript** or **vbscript** code given as value, when there is any event that takes place for any HTML5 element.

We would cover element-specific events while discussing those elements in detail in subsequent chapters.

Attribute	Value	Description
offline	script	Triggers when the document goes offline
onabort	script	Triggers on an abort event
onafterprint	script	Triggers after the document is printed
onbeforeonload	script	Triggers before the document loads
onbeforeprint	script	Triggers before the document is printed
onblur	script	Triggers when the window loses focus
oncanplay	script	Triggers when media can start play, but might has to stop for buffering
oncanplaythrough	script	Triggers when media can be played to the end, without stopping for buffering
onchange	script	Triggers when an element changes
onclick	script	Triggers on a mouse click
oncontextmenu	script	Triggers when a context menu is triggered
ondblclick	script	Triggers on a mouse double-click
ondrag	script	Triggers when an element is dragged
ondragend	script	Triggers at the end of a drag operation
ondragenter	script	Triggers when an element has been dragged to a valid drop target
ondragleave	script	Triggers when an element leaves a valid drop target
ondragover	script	Triggers when an element is being dragged over a valid drop target

ondragstart	script	Triggers at the start of a drag operation
ondrop	script	Triggers when dragged element is being dropped
ondurationchange	script	Triggers when the length of the media is changed
onemptied	script	Triggers when a media resource element suddenly becomes empty.
onended	script	Triggers when media has reach the end
onerror	script	Triggers when an error occur
onfocus	script	Triggers when the window gets focus
onformchange	script	Triggers when a form changes
onforminput	script	Triggers when a form gets user input
onhaschange	script	Triggers when the document has change
oninput	script	Triggers when an element gets user input
oninvalid	script	Triggers when an element is invalid
onkeydown	script	Triggers when a key is pressed
onkeypress	script	Triggers when a key is pressed and released
onkeyup	script	Triggers when a key is released
onload	script	Triggers when the document loads
onloadeddata	script	Triggers when media data is loaded
onloadedmetadata	script	Triggers when the duration and other media data of a media element is loaded
onloadstart	script	Triggers when the browser starts to load the media data
onmessage	script	Triggers when the message is triggered
onmousedown	script	Triggers when a mouse button is pressed
onmousemove	script	Triggers when the mouse pointer moves
onmouseout	script	Triggers when the mouse pointer moves out of an element
onmouseover	script	Triggers when the mouse pointer moves over an element
onmouseup	script	Triggers when a mouse button is released
onmousewheel	script	Triggers when the mouse wheel is being rotated
onoffline	script	Triggers when the document goes offline
onoine	script	Triggers when the document comes online

ononline	script	Triggers when the document comes online
onpagehide	script	Triggers when the window is hidden
onpageshow	script	Triggers when the window becomes visible
onpause	script	Triggers when media data is paused
onplay	script	Triggers when media data is going to start playing
onplaying	script	Triggers when media data has start playing
onpopstate	script	Triggers when the window's history changes
onprogress	script	Triggers when the browser is fetching the media data
onratechange	script	Triggers when the media data's playing rate has changed
onreadystatechange	script	Triggers when the ready-state changes
onredo	script	Triggers when the document performs a redo
onresize	script	Triggers when the window is resized
onscroll	script	Triggers when an element's scrollbar is being scrolled
onseeked	script	Triggers when a media element's seeking attribute is no longer true, and the seeking has ended
onseeking	script	Triggers when a media element's seeking attribute is true, and the seeking has begun
onselect	script	Triggers when an element is selected
onstalled	script	Triggers when there is an error in fetching media data
onstorage	script	Triggers when a document loads
onsubmit	script	Triggers when a form is submitted
onsuspend	script	Triggers when the browser has been fetching media data, but stopped before the entire media file was fetched
ontimeupdate	script	Triggers when media changes its playing position
onundo	script	Triggers when a document performs an undo
onunload	script	Triggers when the user leaves the document
onvolumechange	script	Triggers when media changes the volume, also when volume is set to "mute"
onwaiting	script	Triggers when media has stopped playing, but is expected to resume

5. HTML5 – Web Forms 2.0

Web Forms 2.0 is an extension to the forms features found in HTML4. Form elements and attributes in HTML5 provide a greater degree of semantic mark-up than HTML4 and free us from a great deal of tedious scripting and styling that was required in HTML4.

The <input> element in HTML4

HTML4 input elements use the **type** attribute to specify the data type.HTML4 provides following types –

Type	Description
text	A free-form text field, nominally free of line breaks.
password	A free-form text field for sensitive information, nominally free of line breaks.
checkbox	A set of zero or more values from a predefined list.
radio	An enumerated value.
submit	A free form of button initiates form submission.
file	An arbitrary file with a MIME type and optionally a file name.
image	A coordinate, relative to a particular image's size, with the extra semantic that it must be the last value selected and initiates form submission.
hidden	An arbitrary string that is not normally displayed to the user.
select	An enumerated value, much like the radio type.
textarea	A free-form text field, nominally with no line break restrictions.
button	A free form of button which can initiates any event related to button.

Following is the simple example of using labels, radio buttons, and submit buttons –

```
...
<form action="http://example.com/cgiscript.pl" method="post">

    <p>

        <label for="firstname">first name: </label>
        <input type="text" id="firstname"><br />

        <label for="lastname">last name: </label>
```

```
        <input type="text" id="lastname"><br />


        <label for="email">email: </label>
        <input type="text" id="email"><br>


        <input type="radio" name="sex" value="male"> Male<br>
        <input type="radio" name="sex" value="female"> Female<br>
        <input type="submit" value="send"> <input type="reset">
    </p>
</form>
 ...
```

The <input> element in HTML5

Apart from the above-mentioned attributes, HTML5 input elements introduced several new values for the **type** attribute. These are listed below.

NOTE: Try all the following example using latest version of **Opera** browser.

Type	Description
datetime	A date and time (year, month, day, hour, minute, second, fractions of a second) encoded according to ISO 8601 with the time zone set to UTC.
datetime-local	A date and time (year, month, day, hour, minute, second, fractions of a second) encoded according to ISO 8601, with no time zone information.
date	A date (year, month, day) encoded according to ISO 8601.
month	A date consisting of a year and a month encoded according to ISO 8601.
week	A date consisting of a year and a week number encoded according to ISO 8601.
time	A time (hour, minute, seconds, fractional seconds) encoded according to ISO 8601.
number	It accepts only numerical value. The step attribute specifies the precision, defaulting to 1.
range	The range type is used for input fields that should contain a value from a range of numbers.
email	It accepts only email value. This type is used for input fields that should contain an e-mail address. If you try to submit a simple text, it forces to enter only email address in email@example.com format.
url	It accepts only URL value. This type is used for input fields that should contain a URL address. If you try to submit a simple text, it forces to enter

	only URL address either in http://www.example.com format or in http://example.com format.

HTML5 - datetime

A date and time (year, month, day, hour, minute, second, fractions of a second) encoded according to ISO 8601 with the time zone set to UTC.

Example

```
<!DOCTYPE HTML>
<html>
   <body>

      <form action = "/cgi-bin/html5.cgi" method = "get">
         Date and Time : <input type = "datetime" name = "newinput" />
         <input type = "submit" value = "submit" />
      </form>

   </body>
</html>
```

Output

Date and Time : [   ] submit

HTML5 - datetime local

A date and time (year, month, day, hour, minute, second, fractions of a second) encoded according to ISO 8601, with no time zone information.

Example

```
<!DOCTYPE HTML>
<html>
    <body>

        <form action = "/cgi-bin/html5.cgi" method = "get">
            Local Date and Time : <input type = "datetime-local" name = "newinput" />
            <input type = "submit" value = "submit" />
        </form>


    </body>
</html>
```

Output

Local Date and Time : `mm/dd/yyyy --:-- --` [submit]

HTML5 – date

A date (year, month, day) encoded according to ISO 8601.

Example

```
<!DOCTYPE HTML>
<html>
    <body>

        <form action = "/cgi-bin/html5.cgi" method = "get">
```

```
          Date : <input type = "date" name = "newinput" />
          <input type = "submit" value = "submit" />
        </form>
      </body>
  </html>
```

Output

Date : mm/dd/yyyy   submit

HTML5 – month

A date consisting of a year and a month encoded according to ISO 8601.

Example

```
<!DOCTYPE HTML>
<html>
    <body>

        <form action = "/cgi-bin/html5.cgi" method = "get">
          Month : <input type = "month" name = "newinput" />
          <input type = "submit" value = "submit" />
        </form>

    </body>
</html>
```

Output

Month : [.......... ....] [submit]

HTML5 - week

A date consisting of a year and a week number encoded according to ISO 8601.

Example

```
<!DOCTYPE HTML>
<html>
   <body>

      <form action = "/cgi-bin/html5.cgi" method = "get">
         Week : <input type = "week" name = "newinput" />
         <input type = "submit" value = "submit" />
      </form>

   </body>
</html>
```

Output

Week : [Week --, ----] [submit]

HTML5 – time

A time (hour, minute, seconds, fractional seconds) encoded according to ISO 8601.

Example

```
<!DOCTYPE HTML>
<html>
   <body>

      <form action = "/cgi-bin/html5.cgi" method = "get">
         Time : <input type = "time" name = "newinput" />
         <input type = "submit" value = "submit" />
      </form>

   </body>
</html>
```

Output

HTML5 – number

It accepts only numerical value. The step attribute specifies the precision, defaulting to 1.

Example

```
<!DOCTYPE HTML>
<html>
   <body>

      <form action = "/cgi-bin/html5.cgi" method = "get">
```

```
        Select Number : <input type = "number" min = "0" max = "10" step "1"
           value = "5" name = "newinput" />
        <input type = "submit" value = "submit" />
      </form>


   </body>
</html>
```

Output

Select Number : 5   submit

HTML5 – range

The range type is used for input fields that should contain a value from a range of numbers.

Example

```
<!DOCTYPE HTML>
<html>
   <body>


      <form action = "/cgi-bin/html5.cgi" method = "get">
         Select Range : <input type = "range" min = "0" max = "10" step "1"
            value = "5" name = "newinput" />
         <input type = "submit" value = "submit" />
      </form>


   </body>
</html>
```

Output

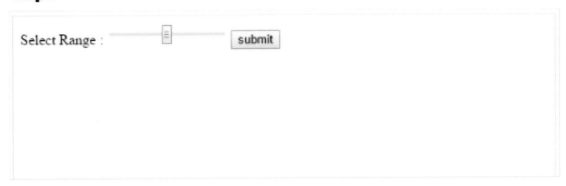

HTML5 - email

It accepts only email value. This type is used for input fields that should contain an e-mail address. If you try to submit a simple text, it forces to enter only email address in email@example.com format.

Example

```
<!DOCTYPE HTML>
<html>
   <body>

      <form action = "/cgi-bin/html5.cgi" method = "get">
         Enter email : <input type = "email" name = "newinput" />
         <input type = "submit" value = "submit" />
      </form>

   </body>
</html>
```

Output

Enter email : ⬚ submit

HTML5 – URL

It accepts only URL value. This type is used for input fields that should contain a URL address. If you try to submit a simple text, it forces to enter only URL address either in **http://www.example.com** format or in **http://example.com** format.

Example

```
<!DOCTYPE HTML>
<html>
   <body>


      <form action = "/cgi-bin/html5.cgi" method = "get">
         Enter URL : <input type = "url" name = "newinput" />
         <input type = "submit" value = "submit" />
      </form>


   </body>
</html>
```

Output

Enter URL : [   ] submit

The <output> element

HTML5 introduced a new element <output> which is used to represent the result of different types of output, such as output written by a script.

You can use the **for** attribute to specify a relationship between the output element and other elements in the document that affected the calculation (for example, as inputs or parameters). The value of the for attribute is a space-separated list of IDs of other elements.

```
<!DOCTYPE HTML>
```

```html
<html>

   <script type="text/javascript">
      function showResult()
      {
         x = document.forms["myform"]["newinput"].value;
         document.forms["myform"]["result"].value=x;
      }
   </script>

   <body>

      <form action="/cgi-bin/html5.cgi" method="get" name="myform">
         Enter a value : <input type="text" name="newinput" />
         <input type="button" value="Result"  onclick="showResult();" />
         <output name="result"/>
      </form>

   </body>

</html>
```

It will produce the following result −

The placeholder attribute

HTML5 introduced a new attribute called **placeholder**. This attribute on <input> and <textarea> elements provide a hint to the user of what can be entered in the field. The placeholder text must not contain carriage returns or line-feeds.

Here is the simple syntax for placeholder attribute −

```
<input type="text" name="search" placeholder="search the web"/>
```

This attribute is supported by latest versions of Mozilla, Safari and Crome browsers only.

```html
<!DOCTYPE HTML>
<html>

    <body>

        <form action="/cgi-bin/html5.cgi" method="get">
            Enter email : <input type="email" name="newinput"
placeholder="email@example.com"/>
            <input type="submit" value="submit" />
        </form>

    </body>

</html>
```

This will produce the following result −

Enter email : email@example.com submit

The autofocus attribute

This is a simple one-step pattern, easily programmed in JavaScript at the time of document load, automatically focus one particular form field.

HTML5 introduced a new attribute called **autofocus** which would be used as follows −

```
<input type="text" name="search" autofocus/>
```

This attribute is supported by latest versions of Mozilla, Safari and Chrome browsers only.

```
<!DOCTYPE HTML>

<html>

    <body>

        <form action="/cgi-bin/html5.cgi" method="get">
            Enter email : <input type="text" name="newinput" autofocus/>
            <p>Try to submit using Submit button</p>
            <input type="submit" value="submit" />
        </form>

    </body>

</html>
```

The required attribute

Now you do not need to have JavaScript for client-side validations like empty text box would never be submitted because HTML5 introduced a new attribute called **required** which would be used as follows and would insist to have a value −

```
<input type="text" name="search" required/>
```

This attribute is supported by latest versions of Mozilla, Safari and Chrome browsers only.

```
<!DOCTYPE HTML>
<html>
    <body>
        <form action="/cgi-bin/html5.cgi" method="get">
            Enter email : <input type="text" name="newinput" required/>
            <p>Try to submit using Submit button</p>
            <input type="submit" value="submit" />
        </form>
    </body>
</html>
```

It will produce the following result −

Enter email : [   ]

Try to submit using Submit button

[submit]

6. HTML5 – SVG

SVG stands for **S**calable **V**ector **G**raphics and it is a language for describing 2D-graphics and graphical applications in XML and the XML is then rendered by an SVG viewer.

SVG is mostly useful for vector type diagrams like Pie charts, Two-dimensional graphs in an X,Y coordinate system etc.

SVG became a W3C Recommendation 14. January 2003 and you can check latest version of SVG specification at **SVG Specification**.

Viewing SVG Files

Most of the web browsers can display SVG just like they can display PNG, GIF, and JPG. Internet Explorer users may have to install the **Adobe SVG Viewer** to be able to view SVG in the browser.

Embedding SVG in HTML5

HTML5 allows embedding SVG directly using **<svg>...</svg>** tag which has following simple syntax −

```
<svg xmlns="http://www.w3.org/2000/svg">
  ...
</svg>
```

Firefox 3.7 has also introduced a configuration option ("about:config") where you can enable HTML5 using the following steps −

- Type **about:config** in your Firefox address bar.

- Click the "I'll be careful, I promise!" button on the warning message that appears (and make sure you adhere to it!).

- Type **html5.enable** into the filter bar at the top of the page.

- Currently it would be disabled, so click it to toggle the value to true.

Now your Firefox HTML5 parser should be enabled and you should be able to experiment with the following examples.

HTML5 – SVG Circle

Following is the HTML5 version of an SVG example which would draw a circle using <circle> tag –

```
<!DOCTYPE html>
<html>
    <head>
        <title>SVG</title>
        <meta charset="utf-8" />
    </head>

    <body>
        <h2>HTML5 SVG Circle</h2>
        <svg id="svgelem" height="200" xmlns="http://www.w3.org/2000/svg">
            <circle id="redcircle" cx="50" cy="50" r="50" fill="red" />
        </svg>
    </body>
</html>
```

This would produce the following result in HTML5 enabled latest version of Firefox.

HTML5 – SVG Rectangle

Following is the HTML5 version of an SVG example which would draw a rectangle using <rect> tag –

```
<!DOCTYPE html>
<html>

    <head>
        <title>SVG</title>
```

```
        <meta charset="utf-8" />
    </head>

    <body>
        <h2>HTML5 SVG Rectangle</h2>
        <svg id="svgelem" height="200" xmlns="http://www.w3.org/2000/svg">
            <rect id="redrect" width="300" height="100" fill="red" />
        </svg>
    </body>
</html>
```

This would produce the following result in HTML5 enabled latest version of Firefox.

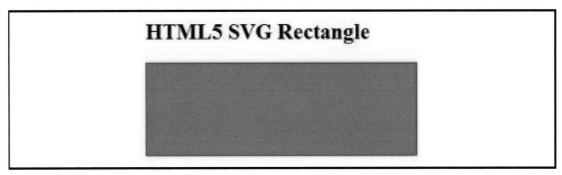

HTML5 – SVG Line

Following is the HTML5 version of an SVG example which would draw a line using <line> tag —

```
<!DOCTYPE html>
<html>

    <head>
        <title>SVG</title>
        <meta charset="utf-8" />
    </head>

    <body>

        <h2>HTML5 SVG Line</h2>

        <svg id="svgelem" height="200" xmlns="http://www.w3.org/2000/svg">
            <line x1="0" y1="0" x2="200" y2="100" style="stroke:red;stroke-width:2"/>
```

```
        </svg>
    </body>
</html>
```

You can use the **style** attribute which allows you to set additional style information like stroke and fill colors, width of the stroke, etc.

This would produce the following result in HTML5 enabled latest version of Firefox.

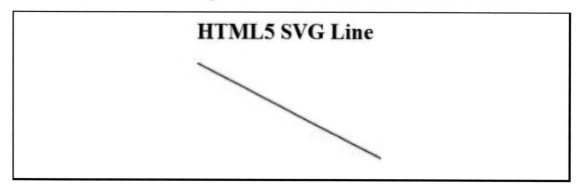

HTML5 – SVG Ellipse

Following is the HTML5 version of an SVG example which would draw an ellipse using <ellipse> tag –

```
<!DOCTYPE html>
<html>
    <head>
        <title>SVG</title>
        <meta charset="utf-8" />
    </head>

    <body>
        <h2>HTML5 SVG Ellipse</h2>
        <svg id="svgelem" height="200" xmlns="http://www.w3.org/2000/svg">
            <ellipse cx="100" cy="50" rx="100" ry="50" fill="red" />
        </svg>

    </body>

</html>
```

This would produce the following result in HTML5 enabled latest version of Firefox.

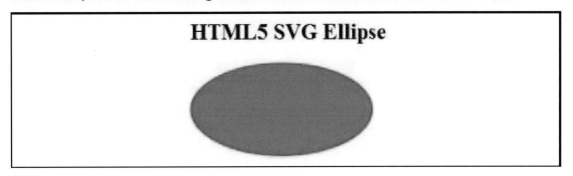

HTML5 – SVG Polygon

Following is the HTML5 version of an SVG example which would draw a polygon using <polygon> tag –

```
<!DOCTYPE html>
<html>
    <head>
        <title>SVG</title>
        <meta charset="utf-8" />
    </head>
    <body>
        <h2>HTML5 SVG Polygon</h2>
        <svg id="svgelem" height="200" xmlns="http://www.w3.org/2000/svg">
            <polygon  points="20,10 300,20, 170,50" fill="red" />
        </svg>
    </body>
</html>
```

This would produce the following result in HTML5 enabled latest version of Firefox.

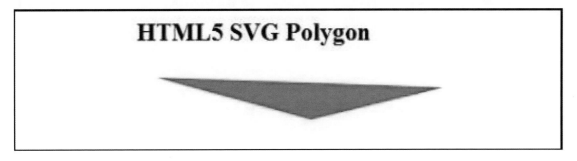

HTML5 – SVG Polyline

Following is the HTML5 version of an SVG example which would draw a polyline using <polyline> tag −

```
<!DOCTYPE html>
<html>

   <head>
      <title>SVG</title>
      <meta charset="utf-8" />
   </head>

   <body>

      <h2>HTML5 SVG Polyline</h2>

      <svg id="svgelem" height="200" xmlns="http://www.w3.org/2000/svg">
         <polyline points="0,0 0,20 20,20 20,40 40,40 40,60" fill="red" />
      </svg>

   </body>

</html>
```

This would produce the following result in HTML5 enabled latest version of Firefox.

HTML5 SVG Polyline

HTML5 – SVG Gradients

Following is the HTML5 version of an SVG example which would draw an ellipse using <ellipse> tag and would use <radialGradient> tag to define an SVG radial gradient.

Similarly, you can use <linearGradient> tag to create SVG linear gradient.

```
<!DOCTYPE html>
<html>
    <head>
        <title>SVG</title>
        <meta charset="utf-8" />
    </head>

    <body>
        <h2>HTML5 SVG Gradient Ellipse</h2>
        <svg id="svgelem" height="200" xmlns="http://www.w3.org/2000/svg">
            <defs>
                <radialGradient id="gradient" cx="50%" cy="50%" r="50%" fx="50%"
fy="50%">
                    <stop offset="0%" style="stop-color:rgb(200,200,200); stop-
opacity:0"/>
                    <stop offset="100%" style="stop-color:rgb(0,0,255); stop-
opacity:1"/>
                </radialGradient>
            </defs>
            <ellipse cx="100" cy="50" rx="100" ry="50" style="fill:url(#gradient)" />
        </svg>
    </body>
</html>
```

This would produce the following result in HTML5 enabled latest version of Firefox.

HTML5 SVG Gradient Ellipse

HTML5 – SVG Star

Following is the HTML5 version of an SVG example which would draw a star using
<polygon> tag.

```
<html>

   <head>

      <style>
         #svgelem{
            position: relative;
            left: 50%;
            -webkit-transform: translateX(-40%);
            -ms-transform: translateX(-40%);
            transform: translateX(-40%);
         }
      </style>

      <title>SVG</title>
      <meta charset="utf-8" />
   </head>
   <body>
      <h2 align="center">HTML5 SVG Star</h2>
      <svg id="svgelem" height="200" xmlns="http://www.w3.org/2000/svg">
         <polygon points="100,10 40,180 190,60 10,60 160,180" fill="red"/>
      </svg>

   </body>
</html>
```

This would produce the following result in HTML5 enabled latest version of Firefox.

7. HTML5 – MathML

The HTML syntax of HTML5 allows for MathML elements to be used inside a document using $...$ tags.

Most of the web browsers can display MathML tags. If your browser does not support MathML, then I would suggest you to use latest version of Firefox.

MathML Examples

Following is a valid HTML5 document with MathML −

```
<!doctype html>
<html>

   <head>
      <meta charset="UTF-8">
      <title>Pythagorean theorem</title>
   </head>

   <body>
      <math xmlns="http://www.w3.org/1998/Math/MathML">
         <mrow>
            <msup><mi>a</mi><mn>2</mn></msup>
            <mo>+</mo>

            <msup><mi>b</mi><mn>2</mn></msup>
            <mo>=</mo>

            <msup><mi>c</mi><mn>2</mn></msup>
         </mrow>
      </math>
   </body>
</html>
```

This will produce the following result −

a2 + b2 = c2

Using MathML Characters

Consider, following is the markup which makes use of the characters ⁢ −

```
<!doctype html>
<html>

    <head>
        <meta charset="UTF-8">
        <title>MathML Examples</title>
    </head>

    <body>

        <math xmlns="http://www.w3.org/1998/Math/MathML">

            <mrow>

                <mrow>

                    <msup>
                        <mi>x</mi>
                        <mn>2</mn>
                    </msup>

                    <mo>+</mo>

                    <mrow>
```

```
                    <mn>4</mn>
                    <mo>⊠</mo>
                    <mi>x</mi>


                </mrow>


                <mo>+</mo>
                <mn>4</mn>


            </mrow>


            <mo>=</mo>
            <mn>0</mn>


        </mrow>


    </math>


  </body>


</html>
```

This would produce the following result. If you are not able to see proper result like x^2 + 4x + 4 = 0, then use Firefox 3.5 or higher version.

This will produce the following result −

x 2 + 4 x + 4 = 0

Matrix Presentation Examples

Consider the following example which would be used to represent a simple 2x2 matrix –

```
<!doctype html>
<html>

    <head>
        <meta charset="UTF-8">
        <title>MathML Examples</title>
    </head>

    <body>
        <math xmlns="http://www.w3.org/1998/Math/MathML">

            <mrow>
                <mi>A</mi>
                <mo>=</mo>

                <mfenced open="[" close="]">

                    <mtable>

                        <mtr>
                            <mtd><mi>x</mi></mtd>
                            <mtd><mi>y</mi></mtd>
                        </mtr>

                        <mtr>
                            <mtd><mi>z</mi></mtd>
                            <mtd><mi>w</mi></mtd>
                        </mtr>

                    </mtable>
                </mfenced>
            </mrow>
        </math>
    </body>
</html>
```

This will produce the following result –

A = x y z w

This would produce the following result. If you are not able to see proper result, then use Firefox 3.5 or higher version.

$$A = \begin{bmatrix} x & y \\ z & w \end{bmatrix}$$

8. HTML5 – Web Storage

HTML5 introduces two mechanisms, similar to HTTP session cookies, for storing structured data on the client side and to overcome following drawbacks.

- Cookies are included with every HTTP request, thereby slowing down your web application by transmitting the same data.

- Cookies are included with every HTTP request, thereby sending data unencrypted over the internet.

- Cookies are limited to about 4 KB of data. Not enough to store required data.

The two storages are **session storage** and **local storage** and they would be used to handle different situations.

The latest versions of pretty much every browser supports HTML5 Storage including Internet Explorer.

Session Storage

The *Session Storage* is designed for scenarios where the user is carrying out a single transaction, but could be carrying out multiple transactions in different windows at the same time.

Example

For example, if a user buying plane tickets in two different windows, using the same site. If the site used cookies to keep track of which ticket the user was buying, then as the user clicked from page to page in both windows, the ticket currently being purchased would "leak" from one window to the other, potentially causing the user to buy two tickets for the same flight without really noticing.

HTML5 introduces the *sessionStorage* attribute which would be used by the sites to add data to the session storage, and it will be accessible to any page from the same site opened in that window, i.e., **session** and as soon as you close the window, the session would be lost.

Following is the code which would set a session variable and access that variable –

```
<!DOCTYPE HTML>
<html>

   <body>

      <script type="text/javascript">
```

```
        if( sessionStorage.hits ){
            sessionStorage.hits = Number(sessionStorage.hits) +1;
        }else{
            sessionStorage.hits = 1;
        }
        document.write("Total Hits :" + sessionStorage.hits );
    </script>

    <p>Refresh the page to increase number of hits.</p>
    <p>Close the window and open it again and check the result.</p>

  </body>

</html>
```

This will produce the following result −

Total Hits :2

Refresh the page to increase number of hits.

Close the window and open it again and check the result.

Local Storage

The *Local Storage* is designed for storage that spans multiple windows, and lasts beyond the current session. In particular, Web applications may wish to store megabytes of user data, such as entire user-authored documents or a user's mailbox, on the client side for performance reasons.

Again, cookies do not handle this case well, because they are transmitted with every request.

Example

HTML5 introduces the *localStorage* attribute which would be used to access a page's local storage area without no time limit and this local storage will be available whenever you would use that page.

Following is the code which would set a local storage variable and access that variable every time this page is accessed, even next time, when you open the window —

```
<!DOCTYPE HTML>
<html>

    <body>

        <script type="text/javascript">

            if( localStorage.hits ){
                localStorage.hits = Number(localStorage.hits) +1;
            }else{
                localStorage.hits = 1;
            }
            document.write("Total Hits :" + localStorage.hits );
        </script>

        <p>Refresh the page to increase number of hits.</p>
        <p>Close the window and open it again and check the result.</p>

    </body>

</html>
```

This will produce the following result —

Total Hits :3

Refresh the page to increase number of hits.

Close the window and open it again and check the result.

Delete Web Storage

Storing sensitive data on local machine could be dangerous and could leave a security hole.

The *Session Storage Data* would be deleted by the browsers immediately after the session gets terminated.

To clear a local storage setting you would need to call **localStorage.remove('key')**; where 'key' is the key of the value you want to remove. If you want to clear all settings, you need to call **localStorage.clear()** method.

Following is the code which would clear complete local storage −

```
<!DOCTYPE HTML>
<html>

    <body>

        <script type="text/javascript">
            localStorage.clear();
            // Reset number of hits.
            if( localStorage.hits ){
                localStorage.hits = Number(localStorage.hits) +1;
            }else{
                localStorage.hits = 1;
            }
            document.write("Total Hits :" + localStorage.hits );

        </script>

        <p>Refreshing the page would not to increase hit counter.</p>
        <p>Close the window and open it again and check the result.</p>

    </body>
</html>
```

This will produce the following result −

Total Hits :1

Refreshing the page would not to increase hit counter.

Close the window and open it again and check the result.

9. HTML5 – Web SQL Database

The Web SQL Database API isn't actually part of the HTML5 specification but it is a separate specification which introduces a set of APIs to manipulate client-side databases using SQL.

I'm assuming you are a great web developer and if that is the case then no doubt, you would be well aware of SQL and RDBMS concepts.

Web SQL Database will work in latest version of Safari, Chrome and Opera.

The Core Methods

There are following three core methods defined in the spec that I am going to cover in this tutorial –

- **openDatabase:** This method creates the database object either using existing database or creating new one.

- **transaction:** This method gives us the ability to control a transaction and performing either commit or rollback based on the situation.

- **executeSql:** This method is used to execute actual SQL query.

Opening Database

The *openDatabase* method takes care of opening a database if it already exists, this method will create it if it already does not exist.

To create and open a database, use the following code –

```
var db = openDatabase('mydb', '1.0', 'Test DB', 2 * 1024 * 1024);
```

The above method took the following five parameters –

- Database name

- Version number

- Text description

- Size of database

- Creation callback

The last and 5th argument, creation callback will be called if the database is being created. Without this feature, however, the databases are still being created on the fly and correctly versioned.

Executing queries

To execute a query you use the database.transaction() function. This function needs a single argument, which is a function that takes care of actually executing the query as follows –

```
var db = openDatabase('mydb', '1.0', 'Test DB', 2 * 1024 * 1024);
db.transaction(function (tx) {
    tx.executeSql('CREATE TABLE IF NOT EXISTS LOGS (id unique, log)');
});
```

The above query will create a table called LOGS in 'mydb' database.

INSERT Operation

To create enteries into the table we add simple SQL query in the above example as follows –

```
var db = openDatabase('mydb', '1.0', 'Test DB', 2 * 1024 * 1024);
db.transaction(function (tx) {
    tx.executeSql('CREATE TABLE IF NOT EXISTS LOGS (id unique, log)');
    tx.executeSql('INSERT INTO LOGS (id, log) VALUES (1, "foobar")');
    tx.executeSql('INSERT INTO LOGS (id, log) VALUES (2, "logmsg")');
});
```

We can pass dynamic values while creating entering as follows –

```
var db = openDatabase('mydb', '1.0', 'Test DB', 2 * 1024 * 1024);

db.transaction(function (tx) {
    tx.executeSql('CREATE TABLE IF NOT EXISTS LOGS (id unique, log)');
    tx.executeSql('INSERT INTO LOGS (id,log) VALUES (?, ?)', [e_id, e_log];
});
```

Here **e_id** and **e_log** are external variables, and executeSql maps each item in the array argument to the "?"s.

READ Operation

To read already existing records we use a callback to capture the results as follows –

```
var db = openDatabase('mydb', '1.0', 'Test DB', 2 * 1024 * 1024);

db.transaction(function (tx) {
    tx.executeSql('CREATE TABLE IF NOT EXISTS LOGS (id unique, log)');
```

```
    tx.executeSql('INSERT INTO LOGS (id, log) VALUES (1, "foobar")');
    tx.executeSql('INSERT INTO LOGS (id, log) VALUES (2, "logmsg")');
});


db.transaction(function (tx) {
    tx.executeSql('SELECT * FROM LOGS', [], function (tx, results) {
        var len = results.rows.length, i;
        msg = "<p>Found rows: " + len + "</p>";
        document.querySelector('#status').innerHTML +=  msg;


        for (i = 0; i < len; i++){
            alert(results.rows.item(i).log );
        }


    }, null);
});
```

Final Example

So finally, let us keep this example in a full-fledged HTML5 document as follows and try to
run it with Safari browser.

```
<!DOCTYPE HTML>
<html>

    <head>

        <script type="text/javascript">

            var db = openDatabase('mydb', '1.0', 'Test DB', 2 * 1024 * 1024);
            var msg;

            db.transaction(function (tx) {
                tx.executeSql('CREATE TABLE IF NOT EXISTS LOGS (id unique, log)');
                tx.executeSql('INSERT INTO LOGS (id, log) VALUES (1, "foobar")');
                tx.executeSql('INSERT INTO LOGS (id, log) VALUES (2, "logmsg")');
                msg = '<p>Log message created and row inserted.</p>';
                document.querySelector('#status').innerHTML =  msg;
            });
```

```
        db.transaction(function (tx) {
           tx.executeSql('SELECT * FROM LOGS', [], function (tx, results) {
              var len = results.rows.length, i;
              msg = "<p>Found rows: " + len + "</p>";
              document.querySelector('#status').innerHTML +=  msg;

              for (i = 0; i < len; i++){
                 msg = "<p><b>" + results.rows.item(i).log + "</b></p>";
                 document.querySelector('#status').innerHTML +=  msg;
              }
           }, null);
        });

     </script>

   </head>

   <body>
      <div id="status" name="status">Status Message</div>
   </body>

</html>
```

This will produce the following result −

Log message created and row inserted.

Found rows: 2

foobar

logmsg

10.   HTML5 – Server Sent Events

Conventional web applications generate events which are dispatched to the web server. For example, a simple click on a link requests a new page from the server.

The type of events which are flowing from web browser to the web server may be called client-sent events.

Along with HTML5, **WHATWG** Web Applications 1.0 introduces events which flow from web server to the web browsers and they are called Server-Sent Events (SSE). Using SSE you can push DOM events continuously from your web server to the visitor's browser.

The event streaming approach opens a persistent connection to the server, sending data to the client when new information is available, eliminating the need for continuous polling.

Server-sent events standardize how we stream data from the server to the client.

Web Application for SSE

To use Server-Sent Events in a web application, you would need to add an <eventsource> element to the document.

The **src** attribute of <eventsource> element should point to an URL which should provide a persistent HTTP connection that sends a data stream containing the events.

The URL would point to a PHP, PERL or any Python script which would take care of sending event data consistently. Following is a simple example of web application which would expect server time.

```
<!DOCTYPE HTML>
<html>

   <head>
      <script type="text/javascript">
         /* Define event handling logic here */
      </script>
   </head>

   <body>

      <div id="sse">
         <eventsource src="/cgi-bin/ticker.cgi" />
      </div>


      <div id="ticker">
```

```
      <TIME>
    </div>


  </body>


</html>
```

Server Side Script for SSE

A server side script should send **Content-type** header specifying the type *text/event-stream* as follows.

```
print "Content-Type: text/event-stream\n\n";
```

After setting Content-Type, server side script would send an **Event:** tag followed by event name. Following example would send Server-Time as event name terminated by a new line character.

```
print "Event: server-time\n";
```

Final step is to send event data using **Data:** tag which would be followed by integer of string value terminated by a new line character as follows —

```
$time = localtime();
print "Data: $time\n";
```

Finally, following is complete ticker.cgi written in Perl —

```
#!/usr/bin/perl


print "Content-Type: text/event-stream\n\n";


while(true){
    print "Event: server-time\n";
    $time = localtime();
    print "Data: $time\n";
    sleep(5);
}
```

Handle Server-Sent Events

Let us modify our web application to handle server-sent events. Following is the final example.

```html
<!DOCTYPE HTML>
<html>

    <head>

        <script type="text/javascript">

document.getElementsByTagName("eventsource")[0].addEventListener("server-time",
eventHandler, false);

            function eventHandler(event)
            {
                // Alert time sent by the server
                document.querySelector('#ticker').innerHTML = event.data;
            }
        </script>

    </head>

    <body>

        <div id="sse">
            <eventsource src="/cgi-bin/ticker.cgi" />
        </div>

        <div id="ticker" name="ticker">
            [TIME]
        </div>

    </body>

</html>
```

Before testing Server-Sent events, I would suggest that you make sure your web browser supports this concept.

11. HTML5 – WebSockets

WebSockets is a next-generation bidirectional communication technology for web applications which operates over a single socket and is exposed via a JavaScript interface in HTML 5 compliant browsers.

Once you get a Web Socket connection with the web server, you can send data from browser to server by calling a **send()** method, and receive data from server to browser by an **onmessage** event handler.

Following is the API which creates a new WebSocket object.

```
var Socket = new WebSocket(url, [protocal] );
```

Here first argument, url, specifies the URL to which to connect. The second attribute, protocol is optional, and if present, specifies a sub-protocol that the server must support for the connection to be successful.

WebSocket Attributes

Following are the attribute of WebSocket object. Assuming we created Socket object as mentioned above –

Attribute	Description
Socket.readyState	The readonly attribute readyState represents the state of the connection. It can have the following values: • A value of 0 indicates that the connection has not yet been established. • A value of 1 indicates that the connection is established and communication is possible. • A value of 2 indicates that the connection is going through the closing handshake. • A value of 3 indicates that the connection has been closed or could not be opened.
Socket.bufferedAmount	The readonly attribute bufferedAmount represents the number of bytes of UTF-8 text that have been queued using send() method.

WebSocket Events

Following are the events associated with WebSocket object. Assuming we created Socket object as mentioned above −

Event	Event Handler	Description
open	Socket.onopen	This event occurs when socket connection is established.
message	Socket.onmessage	This event occurs when client receives data from server.
error	Socket.onerror	This event occurs when there is any error in communication.
close	Socket.onclose	This event occurs when connection is closed.

WebSocket Methods

Following are the methods associated with WebSocket object. Assuming we created Socket object as mentioned above −

Method	Description
Socket.send()	The send(data) method transmits data using the connection.
Socket.close()	The close() method would be used to terminate any existing connection.

WebSocket Example

A WebSocket is a standard bidirectional TCP socket between the client and the server. The socket starts out as a HTTP connection and then "Upgrades" to a TCP socket after a HTTP handshake. After the handshake, either side can send data.

Client Side HTML & JavaScript Code

At the time of writing this tutorial, there are only few web browsers supporting WebSocket() interface. You can try following example with latest version of Chrome, Mozilla, Opera and Safari.

```
<!DOCTYPE HTML>
<html>
   <head>
      <script type="text/javascript">
         function WebSocketTest()
         {
```

```javascript
            if ("WebSocket" in window)
            {
                alert("WebSocket is supported by your Browser!");
                // Let us open a web socket
                var ws = new WebSocket("ws://localhost:9998/echo");

                ws.onopen = function()
                {
                    // Web Socket is connected, send data using send()
                    ws.send("Message to send");
                    alert("Message is sent...");
                };

                ws.onmessage = function (evt)
                {
                    var received_msg = evt.data;
                    alert("Message is received...");
                };

                ws.onclose = function()
                {
                    // websocket is closed.
                    alert("Connection is closed...");
                };

            }
            else

            {
                // The browser doesn't support WebSocket
                alert("WebSocket NOT supported by your Browser!");
            }
        }
    </script>

</head>

<body>
```

```
    <div id="sse">
        <a href="javascript:WebSocketTest()">Run WebSocket</a>
    </div>
  </body>

</html>
```

Install pywebsocket

Before you test above client program, you need a server which supports WebSocket. Download mod_pywebsocket-x.x.x.tar.gz from pywebsocket which aims to provide a Web Socket extension for Apache HTTP Server and install it following these steps.

- Unzip and untar the downloaded file.

- Go inside **pywebsocket-x.x.x/src/** directory.

- $python setup.py build

- $sudo python setup.py install

- Then read document by:

    o $pydoc mod_pywebsocket

This will install it into your python environment.

Start the Server

Go to the **pywebsocket-x.x.x/src/mod_pywebsocket** folder and run the following command –

```
$sudo python standalone.py -p 9998 -w ../example/
```

This will start the server listening at port 9998 and use the **handlers** directory specified by the -w option where our echo_wsh.py resides.

Now using Chrome browser open the html file your created in the beginning. If your browser supports WebSocket(), then you would get alert indicating that your browser supports WebSocket and finally when you click on "Run WebSocket" you would get Goodbye message sent by the server script.

12. HTML5 – Canvas

HTML5 element <canvas> gives you an easy and powerful way to draw graphics using JavaScript. It can be used to draw graphs, make photo compositions or do simple (and not so simple) animations.

Here is a simple <canvas> element which has only two specific attributes **width** and **height** plus all the core HTML5 attributes like id, name and class, etc.

```
<canvas id="mycanvas" width="100" height="100"></canvas>
```

You can easily find that <canvas> element in the DOM using *getElementById()* method as follows −

```
var canvas  = document.getElementById("mycanvas");
```

Let us see a simple example on using <canvas> element in HTML5 document.

```
<!DOCTYPE HTML>
<html>
   <head>
      <style>
         #mycanvas{border:1px solid red;}
      </style>
   </head>

   <body>
      <canvas id="mycanvas" width="100" height="100"></canvas>
   </body>
</html>
```

This will produce the following result −

The Rendering Context

The <canvas> is initially blank, and to display something, a script first needs to access the rendering context and draw on it.

The canvas element has a DOM method called **getContext**, used to obtain the rendering context and its drawing functions. This function takes one parameter, the type of context**2d**.

Following is the code to get required context along with a check if your browser supports <canvas> element —

```
var canvas  = document.getElementById("mycanvas");


if (canvas.getContext){
   var ctx = canvas.getContext('2d');
   // drawing code here
} else {
   // canvas-unsupported code here
}
```

Browser Support

The latest versions of Firefox, Safari, Chrome and Opera all support for HTML5 Canvas but IE8 does not support canvas natively.

You can use **ExplorerCanvas** to have canvas support through Internet Explorer. You just need to include this JavaScript as follows:

```
<!--[if IE]><script src="excanvas.js"></script><![endif]-->
```

HTML5 Canvas Examples

This tutorial covers the following examples related to HTML5 <canvas> element.

Examples	Description
Drawing Rectangles	Learn how to draw rectangle using HTML5 <canvas> element
Drawing Paths	Learn how to make shapes using paths in HTML5 <canvas> element
Drawing Lines	Learn how to draw lines using HTML5 <canvas> element
Drawing Bezier	Learn how to draw Bezier curve using HTML5 <canvas> element

Drawing Quadratic	Learn how to draw quadratic curve using HTML5 <canvas> element
Using Images	Learn how to use images with HTML5 <canvas> element
Create Gradients	Learn how to create gradients using HTML5 <canvas> element
Styles and Colors	Learn how to apply styles and colors using HTML5 <canvas> element
Text and Fonts	Learn how to draw amazing text using different fonts and their size.
Pattern and Shadow	Learn how to draw different patterns and drop shadows.
Canvas States	Learn how to save and restore canvas states while doing complex drawings on a canvas.
Canvas Translation	This method is used to move the canvas and its origin to a different point in the grid.
Canvas Rotation	This method is used to rotate the canvas around the current origin.
Canvas Scaling	This method is used to increase or decrease the units in a canvas grid.
Canvas Transform	These methods allow modifications directly to the transformation matrix.
Canvas Composition	This method is used to mask off certain areas or clear sections from the canvas.
Canvas Animation	Learn how to create basic animation using HTML5 canvas and JavaScript.

HTML5 Canvas - Drawing Rectangles

There are three methods that draw rectangles on the canvas −

Sr.No.	Method and Description
1	fillRect(x,y,width,height) This method draws a filled rectangle.
2	strokeRect(x,y,width,height) This method draws a rectangular outline.
3	clearRect(x,y,width,height) This method clears the specified area and makes it fully transparent

Here x and y specify the position on the canvas (relative to the origin) of the top-left corner of the rectangle and *width* and *height* are width and height of the rectangle.

Example

Following is a simple example which makes use of above mentioned methods to draw a nice rectangle.

```
<!DOCTYPE HTML>
<html>
    <head>

        <style>
           #test {
              width: 100px;
              height:100px;
              margin: 0px auto;
           }
        </style>

        <script type="text/javascript">
           function drawShape(){

               // Get the canvas element using the DOM
               var canvas = document.getElementById('mycanvas');

               // Make sure we don't execute when canvas isn't supported
               if (canvas.getContext){

                  // use getContext to use the canvas for drawing
                  var ctx = canvas.getContext('2d');

                  // Draw shapes
                  ctx.fillRect(25,25,100,100);
                  ctx.clearRect(45,45,60,60);
                  ctx.strokeRect(50,50,50,50);
               }

               else {
                  alert('You need Safari or Firefox 1.5+ to see this demo.');
```

```
            }
        }
    </script>

</head>

<body id="test" onload="drawShape();">
    <canvas id="mycanvas"></canvas>
</body>

</html>
```

The above code would draw the following rectangle —

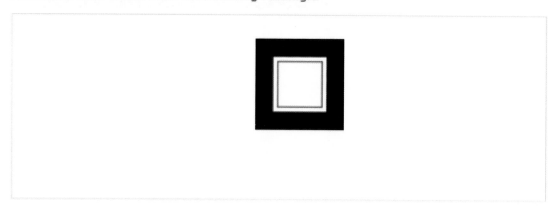

HTML5 Canvas - Drawing Paths

We require the following methods to draw paths on the canvas —

Sr.No.	Method and Description
1	**beginPath()** This method resets the current path.
2	**moveTo(x, y)** This method creates a new subpath with the given point.
3	**closePath()** This method marks the current subpath as closed, and starts a new subpath with a point the same as the start and end of the newly closed subpath.
4	**fill()** This method fills the subpaths with the current fill style.

5	**stroke()**
	This method strokes the subpaths with the current stroke style.
6	**arc(x, y, radius, startAngle, endAngle, anticlockwise)**
	Adds points to the subpath such that the arc described by the circumference of the circle described by the arguments, starting at the given start angle and ending at the given end angle, going in the given direction, is added to the path, connected to the previous point by a straight line.

Example

Following is a simple example which makes use of above mentioned methods to draw a shape.

```html
<!DOCTYPE HTML>
<html>
   <head>

      <style>
         #test {
            width: 100px;
            height:100px;
            margin: 0px auto;
         }
      </style>

      <script type="text/javascript">
         function drawShape(){
            // get the canvas element using the DOM
            var canvas = document.getElementById('mycanvas');

            // Make sure we don't execute when canvas isn't supported
            if (canvas.getContext){
               // use getContext to use the canvas for drawing
               var ctx = canvas.getContext('2d');

               // Draw shapes
               ctx.beginPath();
               ctx.arc(75,75,50,0,Math.PI*2,true);  // Outer circle

               ctx.moveTo(110,75);
```

```
                    ctx.arc(75,75,35,0,Math.PI,false);    // Mouth

                    ctx.moveTo(65,65);
                    ctx.arc(60,65,5,0,Math.PI*2,true);   // Left eye

                    ctx.moveTo(95,65);
                    ctx.arc(90,65,5,0,Math.PI*2,true);   // Right eye

                    ctx.stroke();
                }
                else {
                    alert('You need Safari or Firefox 1.5+ to see this demo.');
                }
            }
        </script>
    </head>

    <body id="test" onload="drawShape();">
        <canvas id="mycanvas"></canvas>
    </body>

</html>
```

It will produce the following output:

HTML5 Canvas - Drawing Lines

Line Methods

We require the following methods to draw lines on the canvas:

Sr.No.	Method and Description

1	**beginPath()** This method resets the current path.
2	**moveTo(x, y)** This method creates a new subpath with the given point.
3	**closePath()** This method marks the current subpath as closed, and starts a new subpath with a point the same as the start and end of the newly closed subpath.
4	**fill()** This method fills the subpaths with the current fill style.
5	**stroke()** This method strokes the subpaths with the current stroke style.
6	**lineTo(x, y)** This method adds the given point to the current subpath, connected to the previous one by a straight line.

Example

Following is a simple example which makes use of the above-mentioned methods to draw a triangle.

```
<!DOCTYPE HTML>
<html>
   <head>

      <style>
         #test {
            width: 100px;
            height:100px;
            margin: 0px auto;
         }
      </style>

      <script type="text/javascript">
         function drawShape(){
            // get the canvas element using the DOM
            var canvas = document.getElementById('mycanvas');

            // Make sure we don't execute when canvas isn't supported
```

```
            if (canvas.getContext){

                // use getContext to use the canvas for drawing
                var ctx = canvas.getContext('2d');
                // Filled triangle
                ctx.beginPath();
                ctx.moveTo(25,25);
                ctx.lineTo(105,25);
                ctx.lineTo(25,105);
                ctx.fill();

                // Stroked triangle
                ctx.beginPath();
                ctx.moveTo(125,125);
                ctx.lineTo(125,45);
                ctx.lineTo(45,125);
                ctx.closePath();
                ctx.stroke();
            }

            else {
                alert('You need Safari or Firefox 1.5+ to see this demo.');
            }
        }
    </script>
  </head>

  <body id="test" onload="drawShape();">
      <canvas id="mycanvas"></canvas>
  </body>
</html>
```

The above example would draw following shape –

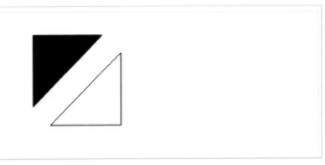

Line Properties

There are several properties which allow us to style lines.

Sr.No.	Property and Description
1	**lineWidth [= value]** This property returns the current line width and can be set, to change the line width.
2	**lineCap [= value]** This property returns the current line cap style and can be set, to change the line cap style. The possible line cap styles are *butt*, *round*, and *square*
3	**lineJoin [= value]** This property returns the current line join style and can be set, to change the line join style. The possible line join styles are *bevel*, *round*, and *miter*.
4	**miterLimit [= value]** This property returns the current miter limit ratio and can be set, to change the miter limit ratio.

Example

Following is a simple example which makes use of *lineWidth* property to draw lines of different width.

```
<!DOCTYPE HTML>
<html>
   <head>

      <style>
         #test {
            width: 100px;
            height:100px;
```

```
            margin: 0px auto;
        }
    </style>

    <script type="text/javascript">
        function drawShape(){
            // get the canvas element using the DOM
            var canvas = document.getElementById('mycanvas');

            // Make sure we don't execute when canvas isn't supported
            if (canvas.getContext){

                // use getContext to use the canvas for drawing
                var ctx = canvas.getContext('2d');

                for (i=0;i<10;i++){
                    ctx.lineWidth = 1+i;
                    ctx.beginPath();
                    ctx.moveTo(5+i*14,5);
                    ctx.lineTo(5+i*14,140);
                    ctx.stroke();
                }
            }

            else
            {
                alert('You need Safari or Firefox 1.5+ to see this demo.');
            }
        }
    </script>
</head>

<body id="test" onload="drawShape();">
    <canvas id="mycanvas"></canvas>
</body>
</html>
```

The above example would draw following shape –

HTML5 Canvas - Drawing Bezier Curves

We need the following methods to draw Bezier curves on the canvas —

Sr.No.	Method and Description
1	beginPath() This method resets the current path.
2	moveTo(x, y) This method creates a new subpath with the given point.
3	closePath() This method marks the current subpath as closed, and starts a new subpath with a point the same as the start and end of the newly closed subpath.
4	fill() This method fills the subpaths with the current fill style.
5	stroke() This method strokes the subpaths with the current stroke style.
6	bezierCurveTo(cp1x, cp1y, cp2x, cp2y, x, y) This method adds the given point to the current path, connected to the previous one by a cubic Bezier curve with the given control points.

The x and y parameters in bezierCurveTo() method are the coordinates of the end point. cp1x and cp1y are the coordinates of the first control point, and cp2x and cp2y are the coordinates of the second control point.

Example

Following is a simple example which makes use of above mentioned methods to draw a Bezier curves.

```
<!DOCTYPE HTML>
<html>
```

```html
<head>

    <style>
        #test {
            width: 100px;
            height:100px;
            margin: 0px auto;
        }
    </style>

    <script type="text/javascript">
        function drawShape(){
            // get the canvas element using the DOM
            var canvas = document.getElementById('mycanvas');

            // Make sure we don't execute when canvas isn't supported
            if (canvas.getContext){

                // use getContext to use the canvas for drawing
                var ctx = canvas.getContext('2d');

                ctx.beginPath();
                ctx.moveTo(75,40);

                ctx.bezierCurveTo(75,37,70,25,50,25);
                ctx.bezierCurveTo(20,25,20,62.5,20,62.5);

                ctx.bezierCurveTo(20,80,40,102,75,120);
                ctx.bezierCurveTo(110,102,130,80,130,62.5);

                ctx.bezierCurveTo(130,62.5,130,25,100,25);
                ctx.bezierCurveTo(85,25,75,37,75,40);

                ctx.fill();
            }

            else {
                alert('You need Safari or Firefox 1.5+ to see this demo.');
```

```
            }
        }
    </script>
  </head>
  <body id="test" onload="drawShape();">
      <canvas id="mycanvas"></canvas>
  </body>
</html>
```

The above example would draw the following shape:

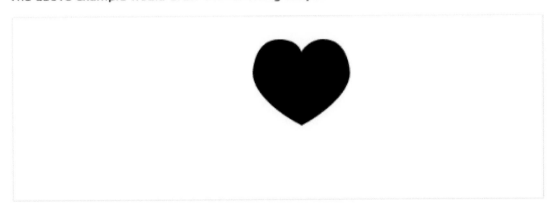

HTML5 Canvas - Drawing Quadratic Curves

We require the following methods to draw quadratic curves on the canvas −

Sr.No.	Method and Description
1	**beginPath()** This method resets the current path.
2	**moveTo(x, y)** This method creates a new subpath with the given point.
3	**closePath()** This method marks the current subpath as closed, and starts a new subpath with a point the same as the start and end of the newly closed subpath.
4	**fill()** This method fills the subpaths with the current fill style.
5	**stroke()** This method strokes the subpaths with the current stroke style.
6	**quadraticCurveTo(cpx, cpy, x, y)**

	This method adds the given point to the current path, connected to the previous one by a quadratic Bezier curve with the given control point.

The x and y parameters in quadraticCurveTo() method are the coordinates of the end point. cpx and cpy are the coordinates of the control point.

Example

Following is a simple example which makes use of above mentioned methods to draw a Quadratic curves.

```html
<!DOCTYPE HTML>
<html>
   <head>

      <style>
         #test {
            width: 100px;
            height:100px;
            margin: 0px auto;
         }
      </style>

      <script type="text/javascript">
         function drawShape(){

            // get the canvas element using the DOM
            var canvas = document.getElementById('mycanvas');

            // Make sure we don't execute when canvas isn't supported
            if (canvas.getContext){

               // use getContext to use the canvas for drawing
               var ctx = canvas.getContext('2d');

               // Draw shapes
```

```
            ctx.beginPath();

            ctx.moveTo(75,25);
            ctx.quadraticCurveTo(25,25,25,62.5);

            ctx.quadraticCurveTo(25,100,50,100);
            ctx.quadraticCurveTo(50,120,30,125);

            ctx.quadraticCurveTo(60,120,65,100);
            ctx.quadraticCurveTo(125,100,125,62.5);

            ctx.quadraticCurveTo(125,25,75,25);
            ctx.stroke();
         }

         else {
            alert('You need Safari or Firefox 1.5+ to see this demo.');
         }
      }
   </script>
</head>

<body id="test" onload="drawShape();">
   <canvas id="mycanvas"></canvas>
</body>

</html>
```

The above example would draw the following shape −

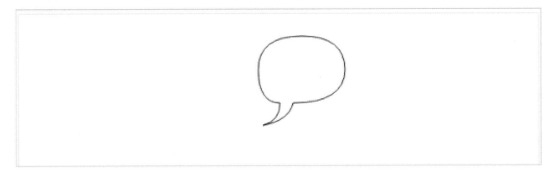

HTML5 Canvas - Using Images

This tutorial would show how to import an external image into a canvas and then how to draw on that image by using following methods —

Sr.No.	Method and Description
1	**beginPath()** This method resets the current path.
2	**moveTo(x, y)** This method creates a new subpath with the given point.
3	**closePath()** This method marks the current subpath as closed, and starts a new subpath with a point the same as the start and end of the newly closed subpath.
4	**fill()** This method fills the subpaths with the current fill style.
5	**stroke()** This method strokes the subpaths with the current stroke style.
6	**drawImage(image, dx, dy)** This method draws the given image onto the canvas. Here *image* is a reference to an image or canvas object. x and y form the coordinate on the target canvas where our image should be placed.

Example

Following is a simple example which makes use of above mentioned methods to import an image.

```
<!DOCTYPE HTML>
<html>
    <head>

        <script type="text/javascript">
            function drawShape(){

                // get the canvas element using the DOM
                var canvas = document.getElementById('mycanvas');

                // Make sure we don't execute when canvas isn't supported
                if (canvas.getContext){
```

```
                // use getContext to use the canvas for drawing
                var ctx = canvas.getContext('2d');

                // Draw shapes
                var img = new Image();
                img.src = '/images/backdrop.jpg';

                img.onload = function(){
                    ctx.drawImage(img,0,0);
                    ctx.beginPath();

                    ctx.moveTo(30,96);
                    ctx.lineTo(70,66);

                    ctx.lineTo(103,76);
                    ctx.lineTo(170,15);

                    ctx.stroke();
                }
            }

            else {
                alert('You need Safari or Firefox 1.5+ to see this demo.');
            }
        }
    </script>
  </head>

  <body onload="drawShape();">
    <canvas id="mycanvas"></canvas>
  </body>

</html>
```

It will produce the following result −

HTML5 Canvas - Create Gradients

HTML5 canvas allows us to fill and stroke shapes using linear and radial gradients using the following methods —

Sr.No.	Method and Description
1	addColorStop(offset, color) This method adds a color stop with the given color to the gradient at the given offset. Here 0.0 is the offset at one end of the gradient, 1.0 is the offset at the other end.
2	createLinearGradient(x0, y0, x1, y1) This method returns a CanvasGradient object that represents a linear gradient that paints along the line given by the coordinates represented by the arguments. The four arguments represent the starting point (x1,y1) and end point (x2,y2) of the gradient.
3	createRadialGradient(x0, y0, r0, x1, y1, r1) This method returns a CanvasGradient object that represents a radial gradient that paints along the cone given by the circles represented by the arguments. The first three arguments define a circle with coordinates (x1,y1) and radius r1 and the second a circle with coordinates (x2,y2) and radius r2.

Linear Gradient Example

Following is a simple example which makes use of above mentioned methods to create Linear gradient.

```
<!DOCTYPE HTML>
<html>
    <head>

        <style>
            #test {
```

```
        width:100px;
        height:100px;
        margin:0px auto;
    }
</style>

<script type="text/javascript">
    function drawShape(){

        // get the canvas element using the DOM
        var canvas = document.getElementById('mycanvas');

        // Make sure we don't execute when canvas isn't supported
        if (canvas.getContext){

            // use getContext to use the canvas for drawing
            var ctx = canvas.getContext('2d');

            // Create Linear Gradients
            var lingrad = ctx.createLinearGradient(0,0,0,150);

            lingrad.addColorStop(0, '#00ABEB');
            lingrad.addColorStop(0.5, '#fff');

            lingrad.addColorStop(0.5, '#66CC00');
            lingrad.addColorStop(1, '#fff');

            var lingrad2 = ctx.createLinearGradient(0,50,0,95);
            lingrad2.addColorStop(0.5, '#000');
            lingrad2.addColorStop(1, 'rgba(0,0,0,0)');

            // assign gradients to fill and stroke styles
            ctx.fillStyle = lingrad;
            ctx.strokeStyle = lingrad2;

            // draw shapes
            ctx.fillRect(10,10,130,130);
            ctx.strokeRect(50,50,50,50);
```

```
                }

            else {
                alert('You need Safari or Firefox 1.5+ to see this demo.');
            }
        }
    </script>
</head>

<body id="test" onload="drawShape();">
    <canvas id="mycanvas"></canvas>
</body>
</html>
```

The above example would produce the following result:

Radial Gradient Example

Following is a simple example which makes use of the above-mentioned methods to create Radial gradient.

```
<!DOCTYPE HTML>
<html>
    <head>

        <style>
            #test {
                width:100px;
                height:100px;
                margin:0px auto;
            }
```

```
        </style>

<script type="text/javascript">
    function drawShape(){

        // get the canvas element using the DOM
        var canvas = document.getElementById('mycanvas');

        // Make sure we don't execute when canvas isn't supported
        if (canvas.getContext){

            // use getContext to use the canvas for drawing
            var ctx = canvas.getContext('2d');

            // Create gradients
            var radgrad = ctx.createRadialGradient(45,45,10,52,50,30);
            radgrad.addColorStop(0, '#A7D30C');
            radgrad.addColorStop(0.9, '#019F62');
            radgrad.addColorStop(1, 'rgba(1,159,98,0)');

            var radgrad2 = ctx.createRadialGradient(105,105,20,112,120,50);
            radgrad2.addColorStop(0, '#FF5F98');
            radgrad2.addColorStop(0.75, '#FF0188');
            radgrad2.addColorStop(1, 'rgba(255,1,136,0)');

            var radgrad3 = ctx.createRadialGradient(95,15,15,102,20,40);
            radgrad3.addColorStop(0, '#00C9FF');
            radgrad3.addColorStop(0.8, '#00B5E2');
            radgrad3.addColorStop(1, 'rgba(0,201,255,0)');

            var radgrad4 = ctx.createRadialGradient(0,150,50,0,140,90);
            radgrad4.addColorStop(0, '#F4F201');
            radgrad4.addColorStop(0.8, '#E4C700');
            radgrad4.addColorStop(1, 'rgba(228,199,0,0)');

            // draw shapes
            ctx.fillStyle = radgrad4;
            ctx.fillRect(0,0,150,150);
```

```
                ctx.fillStyle = radgrad3;
                ctx.fillRect(0,0,150,150);

                ctx.fillStyle = radgrad2;
                ctx.fillRect(0,0,150,150);

                ctx.fillStyle = radgrad;
                ctx.fillRect(0,0,150,150);
            }

            else {
                alert('You need Safari or Firefox 1.5+ to see this demo.');
            }
        }
    </script>
</head>

<body id="test" onload="drawShape();">
    <canvas id="mycanvas"></canvas>
</body>
</html>
```

The above example would produce the following result −

HTML5 Canvas - Styles and Colors

HTML5 canvas provides the following two important properties to apply colors to a shape

Sr.No.	Method and Description
1	**fillStyle** This attribute represents the color or style to use inside the shapes.
2	**strokeStyle** This attribute represents the color or style to use for the lines around shapes

By default, the stroke and fill color are set to black which is CSS color value #000000.

A fillStyle Example

Following is a simple example which makes use of the above-mentioned fillStyle attribute to create a nice pattern.

```
<!DOCTYPE HTML>
<html>
    <head>

        <style>
            #test {
                width: 100px;
                height:100px;
                margin: 0px auto;
            }
        </style>

        <script type="text/javascript">
            function drawShape(){

                // get the canvas element using the DOM
                var canvas = document.getElementById('mycanvas');

                // Make sure we don't execute when canvas isn't supported
                if (canvas.getContext){

                    // use getContext to use the canvas for drawing
                    var ctx = canvas.getContext('2d');

                    // Create a pattern
                    for (var i=0;i<7;i++){
```

```
                for (var j=0;j<7;j++){
                        ctx.fillStyle='rgb(' + Math.floor(255-20.5*i)+ ','+
Math.floor(255 - 42.5*j) + ',255)';
                        ctx.fillRect( j*25, i* 25, 55, 55 );
                    }
                }
            }

            else {
                alert('You need Safari or Firefox 1.5+ to see this demo.');
            }
        }
    </script>
</head>

<body id="test" onload="drawShape();">
    <canvas id="mycanvas"></canvas>
</body>

</html>
```

The above example would produce the following result −

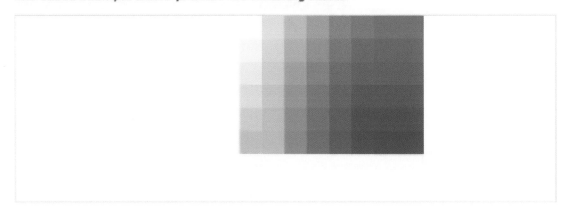

A strokeStyle Example

Following is a simple example which makes use of the above-mentioned fillStyle attribute to create another nice pattern.

```
<!DOCTYPE HTML>
<html>
```

```html
<head>

    <style>
        #test {
            width: 100px;
            height:100px;
            margin: 0px auto;
        }
    </style>
    <script type="text/javascript">
        function drawShape(){

            // get the canvas element using the DOM
            var canvas = document.getElementById('mycanvas');

            // Make sure we don't execute when canvas isn't supported
            if (canvas.getContext){

                // use getContext to use the canvas for drawing
                var ctx = canvas.getContext('2d');

                // Create a pattern
                for (var i=0;i<10;i++){

                    for (var j=0;j<10;j++){
                        ctx.strokeStyle='rgb(255,'+ Math.floor(50-2.5*i)+','+
Math.floor(155 - 22.5 * j ) + ')';
                        ctx.beginPath();

                        ctx.arc(1.5+j*25, 1.5 + i*25,10,10,Math.PI*5.5, true);
                        ctx.stroke();
                    }
                }
            }
            else {
                alert('You need Safari or Firefox 1.5+ to see this demo.');
            }
        }
```

```
        </script>
    </head>
    <body id="test" onload="drawShape();">
        <canvas id="mycanvas"></canvas>
    </body>
</html>
```

The above example would produce the following result −

HTML5 Canvas - Text and Fonts

HTML5 canvas provides capabilities to create text using different font and text properties
listed below −

Sr.No.	Property and Description
1	**font [= value]** This property returns the current font settings and can be set, to change the font.
2	**textAlign [= value]** This property returns the current text alignment settings and can be set, to change the alignment. The possible values are start, end, left, right, andcenter.
3	**textBaseline [= value]** This property returns the current baseline alignment settings and can be set, to change the baseline alignment. The possible values are top, hanging, middle , alphabetic, ideographic and bottom
4	**fillText(text, x, y [, maxWidth])** This property fills the given *text* at the given position indicated by the given coordinates x and y.

5	**strokeText(text, x, y [, maxWidth])** This property strokes the given *text* at the given position indicated by the given coordinates x and y.

Example

Following is a simple example which makes use of above mentioned attributes to draw a text −

```
<!DOCTYPE HTML>
<html>
   <head>

      <style>
         #test {
            width: 100px;
            height:100px;
            margin: 0px auto;
         }
      </style>

      <script type="text/javascript">
         function drawShape(){

            // get the canvas element using the DOM
            var canvas = document.getElementById('mycanvas');

            // Make sure we don't execute when canvas isn't supported
            if (canvas.getContext){

               // use getContext to use the canvas for drawing
               var ctx = canvas.getContext('2d');

               ctx.fillStyle    = '#00F';
               ctx.font         = 'Italic 30px Sans-Serif';
```

```
            ctx.textBaseline = 'Top';
            ctx.fillText  ('Hello world!', 40, 100);


            ctx.font        = 'Bold 30px Sans-Serif';
            ctx.strokeText('Hello world!', 40, 50);
        }


        else {
            alert('You need Safari or Firefox 1.5+ to see this demo.');
        }
      }
    </script>
  </head>

  <body id="test" onload="drawShape();">
    <canvas id="mycanvas"></canvas>
  </body>

</html>
```

The above example would produce the following result −

HTML5 Canvas - Pattern and Shadow

Create Pattern

There is following method required to create a pattern on the canvas −

Sr.No.	Method and Description

	createPattern(image, repetition)
1	This method will use *image* to create the pattern. The second argument could be a string with one of the following values: repeat, repeat-x, repeat-y, andno-repeat. If the empty string or null is specified, repeat will. be assumed

Example

Following is a simple example which makes use of above mentioned method to create a nice pattern.

```html
<!DOCTYPE HTML>
<html>
   <head>

      <style>
         #test {
            width:100px;
            height:100px;
            margin: 0px auto;
         }
      </style>

      <script type="text/javascript">
         function drawShape(){

            // get the canvas element using the DOM
            var canvas = document.getElementById('mycanvas');

            // Make sure we don't execute when canvas isn't supported
            if (canvas.getContext){

               // use getContext to use the canvas for drawing
               var ctx = canvas.getContext('2d');

               // create new image object to use as pattern
               var img = new Image();
```

```
              img.src = 'images/pattern.jpg';
              img.onload = function(){


                  // create pattern
                  var ptrn = ctx.createPattern(img,'repeat');


                  ctx.fillStyle = ptrn;
                  ctx.fillRect(0,0,150,150);
              }
          }
          else {
              alert('You need Safari or Firefox 1.5+ to see this demo.');
          }
       }
    </script>
  </head>
  <body id="test" onload="drawShape();">
      <canvas id="mycanvas"></canvas>
  </body>
</html>
```

Assuming we have following pattern *images/pattern.jpg*.

The above example would draw following result –

Create Shadows

HTML5 canvas provides capabilities to create nice shadows around the drawings. All drawing operations are affected by the four global shadow attributes.

Sr.No.	Property and Description
1	**shadowColor [= value]** This property returns the current shadow color and can be set, to change the shadow color.
2	**shadowOffsetX [= value]** This property returns the current shadow offset X and can be set, to change the shadow offset X.
3	**shadowOffsetY [= value]** This property returns the current shadow offset Y and can be set, change the shadow offset Y.
4	**shadowBlur [= value]** This property returns the current level of blur applied to shadows and can be set, to change the blur level.

Example

Following is a simple example which makes use of above mentioned attributes to draw a shadow.

```
<!DOCTYPE HTML>
<html>
   <head>

      <style>
         #test {
            width: 100px;
            height:100px;
            margin: 0px auto;
         }
      </style>

      <script type="text/javascript">
         function drawShape(){

            // get the canvas element using the DOM
            var canvas = document.getElementById('mycanvas');

            // Make sure we don't execute when canvas isn't supported
            if (canvas.getContext){
```

```
            // use getContext to use the canvas for drawing
            var ctx = canvas.getContext('2d');

            ctx.shadowOffsetX = 2;
            ctx.shadowOffsetY = 2;

            ctx.shadowBlur = 2;
            ctx.shadowColor = "rgba(0, 0, 0, 0.5)";

            ctx.font = "20px Times New Roman";
            ctx.fillStyle = "Black";

            ctx.fillText("This is shadow test", 5, 30);
         }

         else {
            alert('You need Safari or Firefox 1.5+ to see this demo.');
         }
      }
   </script>
</head>

<body id="test" onload="drawShape();">
   <canvas id="mycanvas"></canvas>
</body>

</html>
```

HTML5 Canvas - Save and Restore States

HTML5 canvas provides two important methods to save and restore the canvas states. The canvas drawing state is basically a snapshot of all the styles and transformations that have been applied and consists of the followings −

- The transformations such as translate, rotate and scale etc.

- The current clipping region.

- The current values of the following attributes: strokeStyle, fillStyle, globalAlpha, lineWidth, lineCap, lineJoin, miterLimit, shadowOffsetX, shadowOffsetY, *shadowBlur, shadowColor, globalCompositeOperation, font, textAlign, textBaseline.*

Canvas states are stored on a stack every time the **save** method is called, and the last saved state is returned from the stack every time the **restore** method is called.

Sr.No.	Method and Description
1	**save()** This method pushes the current state onto the stack..
2	**restore()** This method pops the top state on the stack, restoring the context to that state.

Example

Following is a simple example which makes use of above mentioned methods to show how the *restore* is called, to restore the original state and the last rectangle is once again drawn in black.

```
<!DOCTYPE HTML>
<html>
   <head>

      <style>
         #test {
            width: 100px;
            height:100px;
            margin: 0px auto;
         }
      </style>

      <script type="text/javascript">
         function drawShape(){

            // get the canvas element using the DOM
            var canvas = document.getElementById('mycanvas');

            // Make sure we don't execute when canvas isn't supported
```

```javascript
if (canvas.getContext){

    // use getContext to use the canvas for drawing
    var ctx = canvas.getContext('2d');

    //  draw a rectangle with default settings
    ctx.fillRect(0,0,150,150);

    //  Save the default state
    ctx.save();

    // Make changes to the settings
    ctx.fillStyle = '#66FFFF'
    ctx.fillRect( 15,15,120,120);

    // Save the current state
    ctx.save();

    // Make the new changes to the settings
    ctx.fillStyle = '#993333'
    ctx.globalAlpha = 0.5;
    ctx.fillRect(30,30,90,90);

    // Restore previous state
    ctx.restore();

    // Draw a rectangle with restored settings
    ctx.fillRect(45,45,60,60);

    // Restore original state
    ctx.restore();

    // Draw a rectangle with restored settings
    ctx.fillRect(40,40,90,90);
}

else {
    alert('You need Safari or Firefox 1.5+ to see this demo.');
```

```
            }
        }
    </script>
</head>

<body id="test" onload="drawShape();">
    <canvas id="mycanvas"></canvas>
</body>

</html>
```

The above example would produce the following result −

This is shadow test

HTML5 Canvas - Translation

HTML5 canvas provides **translate(x, y)** method which is used to move the canvas and its origin to a different point in the grid.

Here argument x is the amount the canvas is moved to the left or right, and y is the amount it's moved up or down

Example

Following is a simple example which makes use of above method to draw various Spirographs −

```
<!DOCTYPE HTML>
<html>
    <head>

        <style>
            #test {
                width:100px;
```

```
            height:100px;
            margin:0px auto;
        }
    </style>

    <script type="text/javascript">
        function drawShape(){

            // get the canvas element using the DOM
            var canvas = document.getElementById('mycanvas');

            // Make sure we don't execute when canvas isn't supported
            if (canvas.getContext){

                // use getContext to use the canvas for drawing
                var ctx = canvas.getContext('2d');
                ctx.fillRect(0,0,300,300);

                for (i=0;i<3;i++) {
                    for (j=0;j<3;j++) {
                        ctx.save();
                        ctx.strokeStyle = "#FF0066";

                        ctx.translate(50+j*100,50+i*100);
                        drawSpirograph(ctx,10*(j+3)/(j+2),-2*(i+3)/(i+1),10);

                        ctx.restore();
                    }
                }
            }

            else {
                alert('You need Safari or Firefox 1.5+ to see this demo.');
            }
        }

        function drawSpirograph(ctx,R,r,O){
            var x1 = R-O;
```

```
            var y1 = 0;
            var i  = 1;


            ctx.beginPath();
            ctx.moveTo(x1,y1);


            do {
                if (i>20000) break;
                var x2 = (R+r)*Math.cos(i*Math.PI/72) -
(r+O)*Math.cos(((R+r)/r)*(i*Math.PI/72))
                var y2 = (R+r)*Math.sin(i*Math.PI/72) -
(r+O)*Math.sin(((R+r)/r)*(i*Math.PI/72))
                ctx.lineTo(x2,y2);


                x1 = x2;
                y1 = y2;
                i++;
            } while (x2 != R-O && y2 != 0 );
            ctx.stroke();
        }
    </script>
  </head>


  <body id="test" onload="drawShape();">
      <canvas id="mycanvas" width="400" height="400"></canvas>
  </body>
</html>
```

The above example would produce the following result −

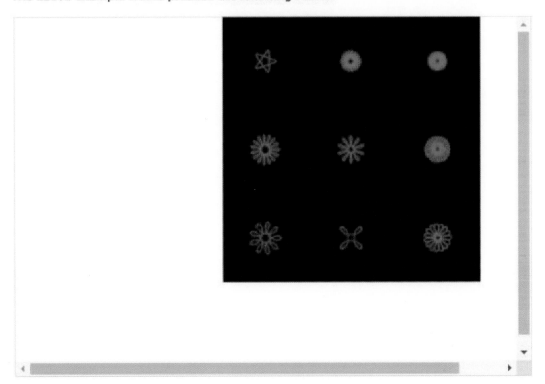

HTML5 Canvas - Rotation

HTML5 canvas provides **rotate(angle)** method which is used to rotate the canvas around the current origin.

This method only takes one parameter and that's the angle the canvas is rotated by. This is a clockwise rotation measured in radians.

Example

Following is a simple example which we are running two loops where first loop determines the number of rings, and the second determines the number of dots drawn in each ring.

```
<!DOCTYPE HTML>
<html>
   <head>

      <style>
         #test {
```

```html
        width: 100px;
        height:100px;
        margin: 0px auto;
    }
</style>
<script type="text/javascript">
   function drawShape(){

        // get the canvas element using the DOM
        var canvas = document.getElementById('mycanvas');

        // Make sure we don't execute when canvas isn't supported
        if (canvas.getContext){

           // use getContext to use the canvas for drawing
           var ctx = canvas.getContext('2d');
           ctx.translate(100,100);

           for (i=1; i<7; i++){
              ctx.save();
              ctx.fillStyle = 'rgb('+(51*i)+','+(200-51*i)+',0)';

              for (j=0; j < i*6; j++){
                 ctx.rotate(Math.PI*2/(i*6));
                 ctx.beginPath();

                 ctx.arc(0,i*12.5,5,0,Math.PI*2,true);
                 ctx.fill();
              }
              ctx.restore();
           }
        }
        else {
           alert('You need Safari or Firefox 1.5+ to see this demo.');
        }
   }
</script>
</head>
```

```
<body id="test" onload="drawShape();">

    <canvas id="mycanvas" width="400" height="400"></canvas>

</body>

</html>
```

The above example would produce the following result –

HTML5 Canvas - Scaling

HTML5 canvas provides **scale(x, y)** method which is used to increase or decrease the units in our canvas grid. This can be used to draw scaled down or enlarged shapes and bitmaps.

This method takes two parameters where x is the scale factor in the horizontal direction and y is the scale factor in the vertical direction. Both parameters must be positive numbers.

Values smaller than 1.0 reduce the unit size and values larger than 1.0 increase the unit size. Setting the scaling factor to precisely 1.0 doesn't affect the unit size.

Example

Following is a simple example which uses spirograph function to draw nine shapes with different scaling factors.

```
<!DOCTYPE HTML>

<html>

    <head>


        <script type="text/javascript">

            function drawShape(){
```

```javascript
// get the canvas element using the DOM
var canvas = document.getElementById('mycanvas');

// Make sure we don't execute when canvas isn't supported
if (canvas.getContext){

  // use getContext to use the canvas for drawing
  var ctx = canvas.getContext('2d');

  ctx.strokeStyle = "#fc0";
  ctx.lineWidth = 1.5;
  ctx.fillRect(0,0,300,300);

  // Uniform scaling
  ctx.save()
  ctx.translate(50,50);
  drawSpirograph(ctx,22,6,5);

  ctx.translate(100,0);
  ctx.scale(0.75,0.75);
  drawSpirograph(ctx,22,6,5);

  ctx.translate(133.333,0);
  ctx.scale(0.75,0.75);
  drawSpirograph(ctx,22,6,5);

  ctx.restore();

  // Non uniform scaling (y direction)
  ctx.strokeStyle = "#0cf";
  ctx.save()
  ctx.translate(50,150);
  ctx.scale(1,0.75);
  drawSpirograph(ctx,22,6,5);

  ctx.translate(100,0);
  ctx.scale(1,0.75);
```

```
        drawSpirograph(ctx,22,6,5);

        ctx.translate(100,0);
        ctx.scale(1,0.75);
        drawSpirograph(ctx,22,6,5);
        ctx.restore();

        // Non uniform scaling (x direction)
        ctx.strokeStyle = "#cf0";
        ctx.save()
        ctx.translate(50,250);
        ctx.scale(0.75,1);
        drawSpirograph(ctx,22,6,5);

        ctx.translate(133.333,0);
        ctx.scale(0.75,1);
        drawSpirograph(ctx,22,6,5);

        ctx.translate(177.777,0);
        ctx.scale(0.75,1);
        drawSpirograph(ctx,22,6,5);

        ctx.restore();
    }

    else {
        alert('You need Safari or Firefox 1.5+ to see this demo.');
    }
}

function drawSpirograph(ctx,R,r,O){
    var x1 = R-O;
    var y1 = 0;
    var i  = 1;

    ctx.beginPath();
    ctx.moveTo(x1,y1);
```

```
            do {

                if (i>20000) break;

                var x2 = (R+r)*Math.cos(i*Math.PI/72) -
(r+O)*Math.cos(((R+r)/r)*(i*Math.PI/72))

                var y2 = (R+r)*Math.sin(i*Math.PI/72) -
(r+O)*Math.sin(((R+r)/r)*(i*Math.PI/72))

                ctx.lineTo(x2,y2);


                x1 = x2;
                y1 = y2;
                i++;

            }


            while (x2 != R-O && y2 != 0 );
            ctx.stroke();

        }
    </script>
  </head>


  <body onload="drawShape();">
      <canvas id="mycanvas" width="400" height="400"></canvas>
  </body>

</html>
```

HTML5 Canvas - Transforms

HTML5 canvas provides methods which allow modifications directly to the transformation matrix. The transformation matrix must initially be the identity transform. It may then be adjusted using the transformation methods.

Sr.No.	Method and Description
1	**transform(m11, m12, m21, m22, dx, dy)** This method changes the transformation matrix to apply the matrix given by the arguments.
2	**setTransform(m11, m12, m21, m22, dx, dy)** This method changes the transformation matrix to the matrix given by the arguments .

The transform(m11, m12, m21, m22, dx, dy) method must multiply the current transformation matrix with the matrix described by −

m11	m21	dx
m12	m22	dy
0	0	1

The *setTransform(m11, m12, m21, m22, dx, dy)* method must reset the current transform to the identity matrix, and then invoke the *transform(m11, m12, m21, m22, dx, dy)* method with the same arguments.

Example

Following is a simple example which makes use of transform() and setTransform() methods −

```
<!DOCTYPE HTML>
<html>
   <head>

      <script type="text/javascript">
         function drawShape(){

            // get the canvas element using the DOM
            var canvas = document.getElementById('mycanvas');

            // Make sure we don't execute when canvas isn't supported
            if (canvas.getContext){

               // use getContext to use the canvas for drawing
               var ctx = canvas.getContext('2d');

               var sin = Math.sin(Math.PI/6);
               var cos = Math.cos(Math.PI/6);

               ctx.translate(200, 200);
               var c = 0;

               for (var i=0; i <= 12; i++) {
                  c = Math.floor(255 / 12 * i);
                  ctx.fillStyle = "rgb(" + c + "," + c + "," + c + ")";
                  ctx.fillRect(0, 0, 100, 100);
```

```
                ctx.transform(cos, sin, -sin, cos, 0, 0);
            }

            ctx.setTransform(-1, 0, 0, 1, 200, 200);
            ctx.fillStyle = "rgba(100, 100, 255, 0.5)";
            ctx.fillRect(50, 50, 100, 100);
        }

        else {
            alert('You need Safari or Firefox 1.5+ to see this demo.');
        }
    }
    </script>
</head>

<body onload="drawShape();">
    <canvas id="mycanvas" width="400" height="400"></canvas>
</body>

</html>
```

The above example would produce the following result −

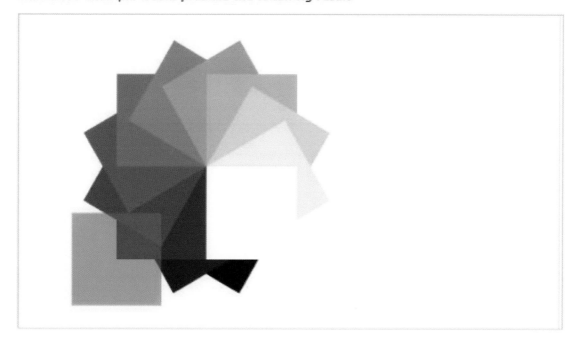

HTML5 Canvas - Composition

HTML5 canvas provides compositing attribute **globalCompositeOperation** which affect all the drawing operations.

We can draw new shapes behind existing shapes and mask off certain areas, clear sections from the canvas using globalCompositeOperation attribute as shown below in the example.

There are following values which can be set for globalCompositeOperation −

Attribute	Description
source-over	This is the default setting and draws new shapes on top of the existing canvas content.
source-in	The new shape is drawn only where both the new shape and the destination canvas overlap. Everything else is made transparent.
source-out	The new shape is drawn where it doesn't overlap the existing canvas content.
source-atop	The new shape is only drawn where it overlaps the existing canvas content.
lighter	Where both shapes overlap the color is determined by adding color values.
xor	Shapes are made transparent where both overlap and drawn normal everywhere else.
destination-over	New shapes are drawn behind the existing canvas content.
destination-in	The existing canvas content is kept where both the new shape and existing canvas content overlap. Everything else is made transparent.
destination-out	The existing content is kept where it doesn't overlap the new shape.
destination-atop	The existing canvas is only kept where it overlaps the new shape. The new shape is drawn behind the canvas content.
darker	Where both shapes overlap the color is determined by subtracting color values.

Example

Following is a simple example which makes use of globalCompositeOperation attribute to create all possible compositions −

```
<!DOCTYPE HTML>
<html>
    <head>
```

```html
<script type="text/javascript">
    var compositeTypes = [
        'source-over','source-in','source-out','source-atop',
        'destination-over','destination-in','destination-out',
        'destination-atop','lighter','darker','copy','xor'
    ];

    function drawShape(){
        for (i=0;i<compositeTypes.length;i++){
            var label = document.createTextNode(compositeTypes[i]);
            document.getElementById('lab'+i).appendChild(label);
            var ctx = document.getElementById('tut'+i).getContext('2d');

            // draw rectangle
            ctx.fillStyle = "#FF3366";
            ctx.fillRect(15,15,70,70);

            // set composite property
            ctx.globalCompositeOperation = compositeTypes[i];

            // draw circle
            ctx.fillStyle = "#0066FF";
            ctx.beginPath();
            ctx.arc(75,75,35,0,Math.PI*2,true);
            ctx.fill();
        }
    }
</script>
</head>

<body onload="drawShape();">
    <table border="1" align="center">
        <tr>
            <td><canvas id="tut0" width="125" height="125"></canvas><br/>
                <label id="lab0"></label>
            </td>

            <td><canvas id="tut1" width="125" height="125"></canvas><br/>
```

```
                <label id="lab1"></label>
        </td>

        <td><canvas id="tut2" width="125" height="125"></canvas><br/>
            <label id="lab2"></label>
        </td>
    </tr>

    <tr>
        <td><canvas id="tut3" width="125" height="125"></canvas><br/>
            <label id="lab3"></label>
        </td>

        <td><canvas id="tut4" width="125" height="125"></canvas><br/>
            <label id="lab4"></label>
        </td>

        <td><canvas id="tut5" width="125" height="125"></canvas><br/>
            <label id="lab5"></label>
        </td>
    </tr>

    <tr>
        <td><canvas id="tut6" width="125" height="125"></canvas><br/>
            <label id="lab6"></label>
        </td>

        <td><canvas id="tut7" width="125" height="125"></canvas><br/>
            <label id="lab7"></label>
        </td>

        <td><canvas id="tut8" width="125" height="125"></canvas><br/>
            <label id="lab8"></label>
        </td>
    </tr>

    <tr>
        <td><canvas id="tut9" width="125" height="125"></canvas><br/>
```

```html
            <label id="lab9"></label>
         </td>

         <td><canvas id="tut10" width="125" height="125"></canvas><br/>
            <label id="lab10"></label>
         </td>

         <td><canvas id="tut11" width="125" height="125"></canvas><br/>
            <label id="lab11"></label>
         </td>
      </tr>
   </table>

   </body>
</html>
```

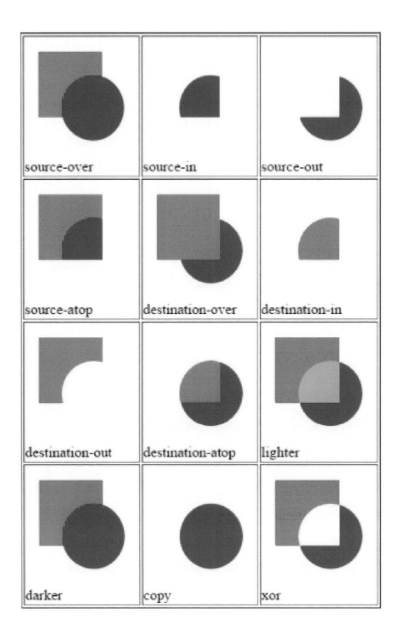

HTML5 Canvas - Animations

HTML5 canvas provides necessary methods to draw an image and erase it completely. We can take Javascript help to simulate good animation over a HTML5 canvas.

Following are the two important Javascript methods which would be used to animate an image on a canvas —

Sr.No.	Method and Description
1	**setInterval(callback, time);** This method repeatedly executes the supplied code after a given *time*milliseconds.

2	**setTimeout(callback, time);** This method executes the supplied code only once after a given *time* milliseconds.

Example

Following is a simple example which would rotate a small image repeatedly −

```
<!DOCTYPE HTML>
<html>
    <head>

        <script type="text/javascript">
            var pattern= new Image();

            function animate(){
                pattern.src = '/html5/images/pattern.jpg';
                setInterval(drawShape, 100);
            }

            function drawShape(){
                // get the canvas element using the DOM
                var canvas = document.getElementById('mycanvas');

                // Make sure we don't execute when canvas isn't supported
                if (canvas.getContext){

                    // use getContext to use the canvas for drawing
                    var ctx = canvas.getContext('2d');

                    ctx.fillStyle = 'rgba(0,0,0,0.4)';
                    ctx.strokeStyle = 'rgba(0,153,255,0.4)';
                    ctx.save();
                    ctx.translate(150,150);

                    var time = new Date();
                    ctx.rotate( ((2*Math.PI)/6)*time.getSeconds() + (
(2*Math.PI)/6000)*time.getMilliseconds() );
                    ctx.translate(0,28.5);
                    ctx.drawImage(pattern,-3.5,-3.5);
```

```
                ctx.restore();
            }

            else {
                alert('You need Safari or Firefox 1.5+ to see this demo.');
            }
        }
    </script>
</head>

<body onload="animate();">
    <canvas id="mycanvas" width="400" height="400"></canvas>
</body>

</html>
```

The above example would produce the following result −

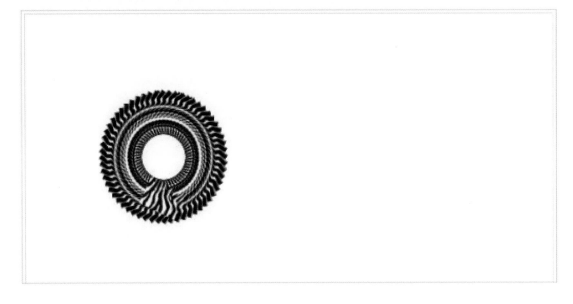

13.   HTML5 – Audio & Video

HTML5 features include native audio and video support without the need for Flash.

The HTML5 <audio> and <video> tags make it simple to add media to a website. You need to set **src** attribute to identify the media source and include a controls attribute so the user can play and pause the media.

Embedding Video

Here is the simplest form of embedding a video file in your webpage:

```
<video src="foo.mp4"  width="300" height="200" controls>
    Your browser does not support the <video> element.
</video>
```

The current HTML5 draft specification does not specify which video formats browsers should support in the video tag. But most commonly used video formats are:

- **Ogg:** Ogg files with Thedora video codec and Vorbis audio codec.

- **mpeg4:** MPEG4 files with H.264 video codec and AAC audio codec.

You can use <source> tag to specify media along with media type and many other attributes. A video element allows multiple source elements and browser will use the first recognized format:

```
<!DOCTYPE HTML>
<html>
<body>
    <video  width="300" height="200" controls autoplay>
        <source src="/html5/foo.ogg" type="video/ogg" />
        <source src="/html5/foo.mp4" type="video/mp4" />
        Your browser does not support the <video> element.
    </video>
</body>
</html>
```

This will produce the following result −

Video Attribute Specification

The HTML5 video tag can have a number of attributes to control the look and feel and various functionalities of the control:

Attribute	Description
autoplay	This Boolean attribute if specified, the video will automatically begin to play back as soon as it can do so without stopping to finish loading the data.
autobuffer	This Boolean attribute if specified, the video will automatically begin buffering even if it's not set to automatically play.
controls	If this attribute is present, it will allow the user to control video playback, including volume, seeking, and pause/resume playback.
height	This attribute specifies the height of the video's display area, in CSS pixels.
loop	This Boolean attribute if specified, will allow video automatically seek back to the start after reaching at the end.
preload	This attribute specifies that the video will be loaded at page load, and ready to run. Ignored if autoplay is present.
poster	This is a URL of an image to show until the user plays or seeks.
src	The URL of the video to embed. This is optional; you may instead use the <source> element within the video block to specify the video to embed
width	This attribute specifies the width of the video's display area, in CSS pixels.

Embedding Audio

HTML5 supports <audio> tag which is used to embed sound content in an HTML or XHTML document as follows.

```
<audio src="foo.wav" controls autoplay>
    Your browser does not support the <audio> element.
</audio>
```

The current HTML5 draft specification does not specify which audio formats browsers should support in the audio tag. But most commonly used audio formats are **ogg, mp3** and **wav**.

You can use <source> tag to specify media along with media type and many other attributes. An audio element allows multiple source elements and browser will use the first recognized format:

```
<!DOCTYPE HTML>
<html>
<body>
    <audio controls autoplay>
        <source src="/html5/audio.ogg" type="audio/ogg" />
        <source src="/html5/audio.wav" type="audio/wav" />
        Your browser does not support the <audio> element.
    </audio>
</body>
</html>
```

This will produce the following result −

Audio Attribute Specification

The HTML5 audio tag can have a number of attributes to control the look and feel and various functionalities of the control:

Attribute	Description
autoplay	This Boolean attribute if specified, the audio will automatically begin to play back as soon as it can do so without stopping to finish loading the data.
autobuffer	This Boolean attribute if specified, the audio will automatically begin buffering even if it's not set to automatically play.
controls	If this attribute is present, it will allow the user to control audio playback, including volume, seeking, and pause/resume playback.
loop	This Boolean attribute if specified, will allow audio automatically seek back to the start after reaching at the end.
preload	This attribute specifies that the audio will be loaded at page load, and ready to run. Ignored if autoplay is present.
src	The URL of the audio to embed. This is optional; you may instead use the <source> element within the video block to specify the video to embed

Handling Media Events

The HTML5 audio and video tag can have a number of attributes to control various functionalities of the control using JavaScript:

Event	Description
abort	This event is generated when playback is aborted.
canplay	This event is generated when enough data is available that the media can be played.
ended	This event is generated when playback completes.
error	This event is generated when an error occurs.
loadeddata	This event is generated when the first frame of the media has finished loading.
loadstart	This event is generated when loading of the media begins.
pause	This event is generated when playback is paused.
play	This event is generated when playback starts or resumes.
progress	This event is generated periodically to inform the progress of the downloading the media.
ratechange	This event is generated when the playback speed changes.

seeked	This event is generated when a seek operation completes.
seeking	This event is generated when a seek operation begins.
suspend	This event is generated when loading of the media is suspended.
volumechange	This event is generated when the audio volume changes.
waiting	This event is generated when the requested operation (such as playback) is delayed pending the completion of another operation (such as a seek).

Following is the example which allows to play the given video:

```
<!DOCTYPE HTML>
<head>
<script type="text/javascript">
function PlayVideo(){
    var v = document.getElementsByTagName("video")[0];
    v.play();
}
</script>
</head>
<html>
<body>
   <form>
   <video  width="300" height="200" src="/html5/foo.mp4">
       Your browser does not support the <video> element.
   </video>
   <input type="button" onclick="PlayVideo();"  value="Play"/>
   </form>
</body>
</html>
```

This will produce the following result –

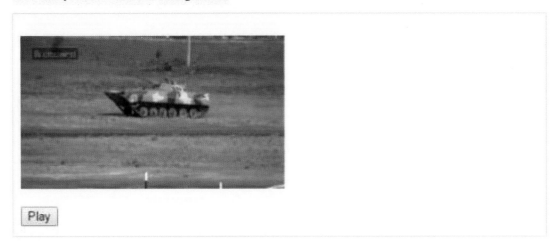

Play

Configuring Servers for Media Type

Most servers don't by default serve Ogg or mp4 media with the correct MIME types, so you'll likely need to add the appropriate configuration for this.

```
AddType audio/ogg .oga

AddType audio/wav .wav

AddType video/ogg .ogv .ogg

AddType video/mp4 .mp4
```

14.   HTML5 – Geolocation

HTML5 Geolocation API lets you share your location with your favorite web sites. A JavaScript can capture your latitude and longitude and can be sent to backend web server and do fancy location-aware things like finding local businesses or showing your location on a map.

Today most of the browsers and mobile devices support Geolocation API. The geolocation APIs work with a new property of the global navigator object ie. Geolocation object which can be created as follows:

```
var geolocation = navigator.geolocation;
```

The geolocation object is a service object that allows widgets to retrieve information about the geographic location of the device.

Geolocation Methods

The geolocation object provides the following methods:

Method	Description
getCurrentPosition()	This method retrieves the current geographic location of the user.
watchPosition()	This method retrieves periodic updates about the current geographic location of the device.
clearWatch()	This method cancels an ongoing watchPosition call.

Example

Following is a sample code to use any of the above method:

```
function getLocation() {
    var geolocation = navigator.geolocation;
    geolocation.getCurrentPosition(showLocation, errorHandler);
}
```

Here showLocation and errorHandler are callback methods which would be used to get actual position as explained in next section and to handle errors if there is any.

Geolocation getCurrentPosition() API

Description

The getCurrentPosition method retrieves the current geographic location of the device. The location is expressed as a set of geographic coordinates together with information about heading and speed. The location information is returned in a Position object.

Syntax

Here is the syntax of this method −

```
getCurrentPosition(showLocation, ErrorHandler, options);
```

Parameters

Here is the detail of parameters −

- **showLocation** − This specifies the callback method that retrieves the location information. This method is called asynchronously with an object corresponding to the **Position** object which stores the returned location information.

- **ErrorHandler** − This optional parameter specifies the callback method that is invoked when an error occurs in processing the asynchronous call. This method is called with the **PositionError** object that stores the returned error information.

- **options** − This optional parameter specifies a set of options for retrieving the location information. You can specify (a) Accuracy of the returned location information (b) Timeout for retrieving the location information and (c) Use of cached location information.

Return value

The getCurrentPosition method does not return a value.

Example

```html
<!DOCTYPE HTML>
<html>
   <head>

      <script type="text/javascript">

         function showLocation(position) {
            var latitude = position.coords.latitude;
            var longitude = position.coords.longitude;
            alert("Latitude : " + latitude + " Longitude: " + longitude);
         }
```

```
        function errorHandler(err) {
            if(err.code == 1) {
                alert("Error: Access is denied!");
            }


            else if( err.code == 2) {
                alert("Error: Position is unavailable!");
            }
        }


        function getLocation(){


            if(navigator.geolocation){
                // timeout at 60000 milliseconds (60 seconds)
                var options = {timeout:60000};
                navigator.geolocation.getCurrentPosition(showLocation,
errorHandler, options);
            }


            else{
                alert("Sorry, browser does not support geolocation!");
            }
        }


    </script>

  </head>
  <body>

    <form>
        <input type="button" onclick="getLocation();" value="Get Location"/>
    </form>

  </body>
</html>
```

Geolocation watchPosition() API

Description

The watchPosition method retrieves periodic updates about the current geographic location of the device. The location is expressed as a set of geographic coordinates together with information about heading and speed.

The location information is returned in a Position object. Each update returns a new Position object.

Syntax

Here is the syntax of this method −

```
watchPosition(showLocation, ErrorHandler, options);
```

Parameters

Here is the detail of parameters −

- **showLocation** − This specifies the callback method that retrieves the location information. This method is called asynchronously with an object corresponding to the **Position** object which stores the returned location information.

- **ErrorHandler** − This optional parameter specifies the callback method that is invoked when an error occurs in processing the asynchronous call. This method is called with the **PositionError** object that stores the returned error information.

- **options** − This optional parameter specifies a set of options for retrieving the location information. You can specify (a) Accuracy of the returned location information (b) Timeout for retrieving the location information and (c) Use of cached location information.

Return value

The watchPosition method returns a unique transaction ID (number) associated with the asynchronous call. Use this ID to cancel the watchPosition call and to stop receiving location updates.

Example

```html
<!DOCTYPE HTML>
<head>
    <html>

        <script type="text/javascript">
            var watchID;
            var geoLoc;
```

```javascript
        function showLocation(position) {
           var latitude = position.coords.latitude;
           var longitude = position.coords.longitude;
           alert("Latitude : " + latitude + " Longitude: " + longitude);
        }


        function errorHandler(err) {
           if(err.code == 1) {
              alert("Error: Access is denied!");
           }


           else if( err.code == 2) {
              alert("Error: Position is unavailable!");
           }
        }


        function getLocationUpdate(){
           if(navigator.geolocation){
              // timeout at 60000 milliseconds (60 seconds)
              var options = {timeout:60000};
              geoLoc = navigator.geolocation;
              watchID = geoLoc.watchPosition(showLocation, errorHandler, options);
           }


           else{
              alert("Sorry, browser does not support geolocation!");
           }
        }
     </script>


  </head>
  <body>


     <form>
        <input type="button" onclick="getLocationUpdate();" value="Watch
Update"/>
     </form>
```

```
    </body>
</html>
```

This will produce the following result -

Geolocation clearWatch() API

Description

The clearWatch method cancels an ongoing watchPosition call. When cancelled, the watchPosition call stops retrieving updates about the current geographic location of the device.

Syntax

Here is the syntax of this method —

```
clearWatch(watchId);
```

Parameters

Here is the detail of parameters —

- **watchId** — This specifies the unique ID of the watchPosition call to cancel. The ID is returned by the watchPosition call.

Return value

The clearWatch method does not return a value.

Example

```
<!DOCTYPE HTML>
<html>
    <head>
```

```html
<script type="text/javascript">
   var watchID;
   var geoLoc;

   function showLocation(position) {
      var latitude = position.coords.latitude;
      var longitude = position.coords.longitude;
      alert("Latitude : " + latitude + " Longitude: " + longitude);
   }

   function errorHandler(err) {
      if(err.code == 1) {
         alert("Error: Access is denied!");
      }

      else if( err.code == 2) {
         alert("Error: Position is unavailable!");
      }
   }

   function getLocationUpdate(){
      if(navigator.geolocation){
         // timeout at 60000 milliseconds (60 seconds)
         var options = {timeout:60000};
         geoLoc = navigator.geolocation;
         watchID = geoLoc.watchPosition(showLocation, errorHandler, options);
      }

      else{
         alert("Sorry, browser does not support geolocation!");
      }
   }

   function stopWatch(){
      geoLoc.clearWatch(watchID);
   }
</script>
```

```
    </head>
    <body>


        <form>
            <input type="button" onclick="getLocationUpdate();" value="Watch
Update"/>
            <input type="button" onclick="stopWatch();" value="Stop Watch"/>
        </form>


    </body>
</html>
```

This will produce the following result −

Location Properties

Geolocation methods getCurrentPosition() and getPositionUsingMethodName() specify the callback method that retrieves the location information. These methods are called asynchronously with an object **Position** which stores the complete location information.

The **Position** object specifies the current geographic location of the device. The location is expressed as a set of geographic coordinates together with information about heading and speed.

The following table describes the properties of the Position object. For the optional properties if the system cannot provide a value, the value of the property is set to null.

Property	Type	Description
coords	objects	Specifies the geographic location of the device. The location is expressed as a set of geographic coordinates together with information about heading and speed.

coords.latitude	Number	Specifies the latitude estimate in decimal degrees. The value range is [-90.00, +90.00].
coords.longitude	Number	Specifies the longitude estimate in decimal degrees. The value range is [-180.00, +180.00].
coords.altitude	Number	[Optional] Specifies the altitude estimate in meters above the WGS 84 ellipsoid.
coords.accuracy	Number	[Optional] Specifies the accuracy of the latitude and longitude estimates in meters.
coords.altitudeAccuracy	Number	[Optional] Specifies the accuracy of the altitude estimate in meters.
coords.heading	Number	[Optional] Specifies the device's current direction of movement in degrees counting clockwise relative to true north.
coords.speed	Number	[Optional] Specifies the device's current ground speed in meters per second.
timestamp	date	Specifies the time when the location information was retrieved and the Position object created.

Example

Following is a sample code which makes use of Position object. Here showLocation method is a callback method:

```
function showLocation( position ) {
   var latitude = position.coords.latitude;
   var longitude = position.coords.longitude;
   ...
}
```

Handling Errors

Geolocation is complicated, and it is very much required to catch any error and handle it gracefully.

The geolocations methods getCurrentPosition() and watchPosition() make use of an error handler callback method which gives **PositionError** object. This object has following two properties:

Property	Type	Description
code	Number	Contains a numeric code for the error.
message	String	Contains a human-readable description of the error.

The following table describes the possible error codes returned in the PositionError object.

Code	Constant	Description
0	UNKNOWN_ERROR	The method failed to retrieve the location of the device due to an unknown error.
1	PERMISSION_DENIED	The method failed to retrieve the location of the device because the application does not have permission to use the Location Service.
2	POSITION_UNAVAILABLE	The location of the device could not be determined.
3	TIMEOUT	The method was unable to retrieve the location information within the specified maximum timeout interval.

Example

Following is a sample code which makes use of PositionError object. Here errorHandler method is a callback method:

```
function errorHandler( err ) {
  if (err.code == 1) {
    // access is denied
  }
  ...
}
```

Position Options

Following is the actual syntax of getCurrentPosition() method:

```
getCurrentPosition(callback, ErrorCallback, options)
```

Here third argument is the **PositionOptions** object which specifies a set of options for retrieving the geographic location of the device.

Following are the options which can be specified as third argument:

Property	Type	Description
enableHighAccuracy	Boolean	Specifies whether the widget wants to receive the most accurate location estimate possible. By default this is false.
timeout	Number	The timeout property is the number of milliseconds your web application is willing to wait for a position.

maximumAge	Number	Specifies the expiry time in milliseconds for cached location information.

Example

Following is a sample code which shows how to use above mentioned methods:

```
function getLocation() {
    var geolocation = navigator.geolocation;
    geolocation.getCurrentPosition(showLocation, errorHandler,
                                {maximumAge: 75000});
}
```

15.   HTML5 – Microdata

Microdata is a standardized way to provide additional semantics in your web pages.

Microdata lets you define your own customized elements and start embedding custom properties in your web pages. At a high level, microdata consists of a group of name-value pairs.

The groups are called **items**, and each name-value pair is a **property**. Items and properties are represented by regular elements.

Example

- To create an item, the **itemscope** attribute is used.

- To add a property to an item, the **itemprop** attribute is used on one of the item's descendants.

Here there are two items, each of which has the property "name":

```
<html>
   <body>
      <div itemscope>
         <p>My name is <span itemprop="name">Zara</span>.</p>
      </div>


      <div itemscope>
         <p>My name is <span itemprop="name">Nuha</span>.</p>
      </div>
   </body>
</html>
```

It will produce the following result –

My name is Zara.

My name is Nuha.

Properties generally have values that are strings but it can have following data types:

Global Attributes

Microdata introduces five global attributes which would be available for any element to use and give context for machines about your data.

Attribute	Description
itemscope	This is used to create an item. The itemscope attribute is a Boolean attribute that tells that there is Microdata on this page, and this is where it starts.
itemtype	This attribute is a valid URL which defines the item and provides the context for the properties.
itemid	This attribute is global identifier for the item.
itemprop	This attribute defines a property of the item.
itemref	This attribute gives a list of additional elements to crawl to find the name-value pairs of the item.

Properties Datatypes

Properties generally have values that are strings as mentioned in above example but they can also have values that are URLs. Following example has one property, "image", whose value is a URL:

```
<div itemscope>
  <img itemprop="image" src="tp-logo.gif" alt="TutorialsPoint">
</div>
```

Properties can also have values that are dates, times, or dates and times. This is achieved using the **time** element and its **datetime** attribute.

```
<html>
   <body>

      <div itemscope>
         My birthday is:
         <time itemprop="birthday" datetime="1971-05-08">
            Aug 5th 1971
         </time>

      </div>
   </body>
</html>
```

It will produce the following result −

My birthday is: Aug 5th 1971

Properties can also themselves be groups of name-value pairs, by putting the itemscope attribute on the element that declares the property.

Microdata API support

If a browser supports the HTML5 microdata API, there will be a getItems() function on the global document object. If browser doesn't support microdata, the getItems() function will be undefined.

```
function supports_microdata_api() {
    return !!document.getItems;
}
```

Modernizr does not yet support checking for the microdata API, so you'll need to use the function like the one listed above.

The HTML5 microdata standard includes both HTML markup (primarily for search engines) and a set of DOM functions (primarily for browsers).

You can include microdata markup in your web pages, and search engines that don't understand the microdata attributes will just ignore them. But if you need to access or manipulate microdata through the DOM, you'll need to check whether the browser supports the microdata DOM API.

Defining Microdata Vocabulary

To define microdata vocabulary you need a namespace URL which points to a working web page. For example http://data-vocabulary.org/Person can be used as the namespace for a personal microdata vocabulary with the following named properties:

- **name** - Person name as a simple string

- **Photo** - A URL to a picture of the person.

- **URL** - A website belonging to the person.

Using about properties a person microdata could be as follows:

```
<html>
    <body>

        <div itemscope>
            <section itemscope itemtype="http://data-vocabulary.org/Person">
                <h1 itemprop="name">Gopal K Varma</h1>

                <p>
                    <img itemprop="photo"
src="http://www.zahidserver.runhosting.net/green/images/logo.png">
                </p>

                <a itemprop="url" href="#">Site</a>
            </section>
        </div>

    </body>
</html>
```

It will produce the following result –

Gopal K Varma

Site

Google supports microdata as part of their Rich Snippets program. When Google's web crawler parses your page and finds microdata properties that conform to the http://data-vocabulary.org/Person vocabulary, it parses out those properties and stores them alongside the rest of the page data.

16.   HTML5 – Drag & drop

Drag and Drop (DnD) is powerful User Interface concept which makes it easy to copy, reorder and deletion of items with the help of mouse clicks. This allows the user to click and hold the mouse button down over an element, drag it to another location, and release the mouse button to drop the element there.

To achieve drag and drop functionality with traditional HTML4, developers would either have to either have to use complex JavaScript programming or other JavaScript frameworks like jQuery etc.

Now HTML 5 came up with a Drag and Drop (DnD) API that brings native DnD support to the browser making it much easier to code up.

HTML 5 DnD is supported by all the major browsers like Chrome, Firefox 3.5 and Safari 4 etc.

Drag and Drop Events

There are number of events which are fired during various stages of the drag and drop operation. These events are listed below:

Events	Description
dragstart	Fires when the user starts dragging of the object.
dragenter	Fired when the mouse is first moved over the target element while a drag is occurring. A listener for this event should indicate whether a drop is allowed over this location. If there are no listeners, or the listeners perform no operations, then a drop is not allowed by default.
dragover	This event is fired as the mouse is moved over an element when a drag is occurring. Much of the time, the operation that occurs during a listener will be the same as the dragenter event.
dragleave	This event is fired when the mouse leaves an element while a drag is occurring. Listeners should remove any highlighting or insertion markers used for drop feedback.
drag	Fires every time the mouse is moved while the object is being dragged.
drop	The drop event is fired on the element where the drop was occurred at the end of the drag operation. A listener would be responsible for retrieving the data being dragged and inserting it at the drop location.
dragend	Fires when the user releases the mouse button while dragging an object.

Note: Note that only drag events are fired; mouse events such as *mousemove* are not fired during a drag operation.

The DataTransfer Object:

The event listener methods for all the drag and drop events accept **Event** object which has a readonly attribute called **dataTransfer**.

The **event.dataTransfer** returns **DataTransfer** object associated with the event as follows:

```
function EnterHandler(event) {

    DataTransfer dt = event.dataTransfer;

    . . . . . . . . . . . . .

}
```

The *DataTransfer* object holds data about the drag and drop operation. This data can be retrieved and set in terms of various attributes associated with DataTransfer object as explained below:

S.N.	DataTransfer attributes and their description
1	**dataTransfer.dropEffect [= value]** • Returns the kind of operation that is currently selected. • This attribute can be set, to change the selected operation. • The possible values are none, copy, link, and move.
2	**dataTransfer.effectAllowed [= value]** • Returns the kinds of operations that are to be allowed. • This attribute can be set, to change the allowed operations. • The possible values are **none, copy, copyLink, copyMove, link, linkMove, move, all and uninitialized**.
3	**dataTransfer.types** Returns a DOMStringList listing the formats that were set in the dragstart event. In addition, if any files are being dragged, then one of the types will be the string "Files".
4	**dataTransfer.clearData ([format])** Removes the data of the specified formats. Removes all data if the argument is omitted.
5	**dataTransfer.setData(format, data)** Adds the specified data.
6	**data = dataTransfer.getData(format)** Returns the specified data. If there is no such data, returns the empty string.
7	**dataTransfer.files** Returns a FileList of the files being dragged, if any.
8	**dataTransfer.setDragImage(element, x, y)**

	Uses the given element to update the drag feedback, replacing any previously specified feedback.
9	**dataTransfer.addElement(element)** Adds the given element to the list of elements used to render the drag feedback.

Drag and Drop Process

Following are the steps to be carried out to implement Drag and Drop operation:

Step 1: Making an Object Draggable

Here are steps to be taken:

- If you want to drag an element, you need to set the **draggable** attribute to **true** for that element.

- Set an event listener for **dragstart** that stores the data being dragged.

- The event listener **dragstart** will set the allowed effects (copy, move, link, or some combination).

Following is the example to make an object draggable:

```
<!DOCTYPE HTML>
<html>
<head>
<style type="text/css">
#boxA, #boxB {
    float:left;padding:10px;margin:10px; -moz-user-select:none;
}
#boxA { background-color: #6633FF; width:75px; height:75px;   }
#boxB { background-color: #FF6699; width:150px; height:150px; }
</style>
<script type="text/javascript">
function dragStart(ev) {
    ev.dataTransfer.effectAllowed='move';
    ev.dataTransfer.setData("Text", ev.target.getAttribute('id'));
    ev.dataTransfer.setDragImage(ev.target,0,0);
    return true;
}
</script>
</head>
```

```
<body>
<center>
<h2>Drag and drop HTML5 demo</h2>
<div>Try to drag the purple box around.</div>

<div id="boxA" draggable="true"
        ondragstart="return dragStart(event)">
  <p>Drag Me</p>
</div>
<div id="boxB">Dustbin</div>
</center>
</body>
</html>
```

This will produce the following result −

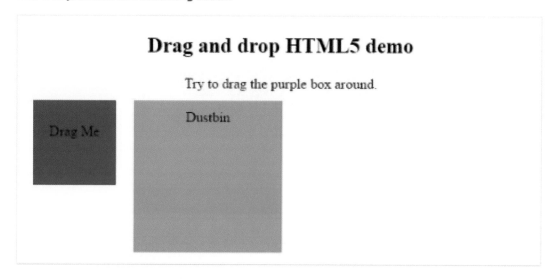

Drag and drop HTML5 demo

Try to drag the purple box around.

Drag Me

Dustbin

Step 2: Dropping the Object

To accept a drop, the drop target has to listen to at least three events.

- The **dragenter** event, which is used to determine whether or not the drop target is to accept the drop. If the drop is to be accepted, then this event has to be canceled.

- The **dragover** event, which is used to determine what feedback is to be shown to the user. If the event is canceled, then the feedback (typically the cursor) is updated based on the dropEffect attribute's value.

- Finally, the **drop** event, which allows the actual drop to be performed.

Following is the example to drop an object into another object:

```
<!DOCTYPE HTML>
<html>
<head>
<style type="text/css">
#boxA, #boxB {
    float:left;padding:10px;margin:10px;-moz-user-select:none;
}
#boxA { background-color: #6633FF; width:75px; height:75px;  }
#boxB { background-color: #FF6699; width:150px; height:150px; }
</style>
<script type="text/javascript">
function dragStart(ev) {
    ev.dataTransfer.effectAllowed='move';
    ev.dataTransfer.setData("Text", ev.target.getAttribute('id'));
    ev.dataTransfer.setDragImage(ev.target,0,0);
    return true;
}
function dragEnter(ev) {
    event.preventDefault();
    return true;
}
function dragOver(ev) {
    return false;
}
function dragDrop(ev) {
    var src = ev.dataTransfer.getData("Text");
    ev.target.appendChild(document.getElementById(src));
    ev.stopPropagation();
    return false;
}
</script>
</head>
<body>
<center>
<h2>Drag and drop HTML5 demo</h2>
<div>Try to move the purple box into the pink box.</div>

<div id="boxA" draggable="true"
```

```
        ondragstart="return dragStart(event)">
    <p>Drag Me</p>
</div>
<div id="boxB" ondragenter="return dragEnter(event)"
    ondrop="return dragDrop(event)"
    ondragover="return dragOver(event)">Dustbin</div>
</center>
</body>
</html>
```

This will produce the following result –

Drag and drop HTML5 demo

Try to move the purple box into the pink box.

17.   HTML5 – Web Workers

JavaScript was designed to run in a single-threaded environment, meaning multiple scripts cannot run at the same time. Consider a situation where you need to handle UI events, query and process large amounts of API data, and manipulate the DOM.

JavaScript will hang your browser in situation where CPU utilization is high. Let us take a simple example where JavaScript goes through a big loop:

```
<!DOCTYPE HTML>
<html>
<head>
<title>Big for loop</title>
  <script>
      function bigLoop(){
          for (var i = 0; i <= 10000000000; i += 1){
             var j = i;
          }
          alert("Completed " + j + "iterations" );
      }
      function sayHello(){
          alert("Hello sir...." );
      }
  </script>
</head>
<body>
   <input type="button" onclick="bigLoop();" value="Big Loop" />
   <input type="button" onclick="sayHello();" value="Say Hello" />
</body>
</html>
```

It will produce the following result –

When you click *Big Loop* button it displays following result in Firefox:

What is Web Workers?

The situation explained above can be handled using **Web Workers** who will do all the computationally expensive tasks without interrupting the user interface and typically run on separate threads.

Web Workers allow for long-running scripts that are not interrupted by scripts that respond to clicks or other user interactions, and allows long tasks to be executed without yielding to keep the page responsive.

Web Workers are background scripts and they are relatively heavy-weight, and are not intended to be used in large numbers. For example, it would be inappropriate to launch one worker for each pixel of a four megapixel image.

When a script is executing inside a Web Worker it cannot access the web page's window object (window.document), which means that Web Workers don't have direct access to the web page and the DOM API. Although Web Workers cannot block the browser UI, they can still consume CPU cycles and make the system less responsive.

How Web Workers Work?

Web Workers are initialized with the URL of a JavaScript file, which contains the code the worker will execute. This code sets event listeners and communicates with the script that spawned it from the main page. Following is the simple syntax:

```
var worker = new Worker('bigLoop.js');
```

If the specified javascript file exists, the browser will spawn a new worker thread, which is downloaded asynchronously. If the path to your worker returns an 404 error, the worker will fail silently.

If your application has multiple supporting JavaScript files, you can import them **importScripts()** method which takes file name(s) as argument separated by comma as follows:

```
importScripts("helper.js", "anotherHelper.js");
```

Once the Web Worker is spawned, communication between web worker and its parent page is done using the **postMessage()** method. Depending on your browser/version, postMessage() can accept either a string or JSON object as its single argument.

Message passed by Web Worker is accessed using **onmessage** event in the main page. Now let us write our bigLoop example using Web Worker. Below is the main page (hello.htm) which will spawn a web worker to execute the loop and to return the final value of variable**j**:

```html
<!DOCTYPE HTML>
<html>
<head>
<title>Big for loop</title>
  <script>
      var worker = new Worker('bigLoop.js');
      worker.onmessage = function (event) {
        alert("Completed " + event.data + "iterations" );
      };

      function sayHello(){
         alert("Hello sir...." );
      }
  </script>
</head>
<body>
   <input type="button" onclick="sayHello();" value="Say Hello"/>
</body>
```

```
</html>
```

Following is the content of bigLoop.js file. This makes use of **postMessage()** API to pass the communication back to main page:

```
for (var i = 0; i <= 1000000000; i += 1){
    var j = i;
}
postMessage(j);
```

This will produce the following result –

```
Say Hello
```

Stopping Web Workers

Web Workers don't stop by themselves but the page that started them can stop them by calling **terminate()** method.

```
worker.terminate();
```

A terminated Web Worker will no longer respond to messages or perform any additional computations. You cannot restart a worker; instead, you can create a new worker using the same URL.

Handling Errors

The following shows an example of an error handling function in a Web Worker JavaScript file that logs errors to the console. With error handling code, above example would become as following:

```
<!DOCTYPE HTML>
<html>
<head>
<title>Big for loop</title>
  <script>
      var worker = new Worker('bigLoop.js');
```

```
      worker.onmessage = function (event) {
        alert("Completed " + event.data + "iterations" );
      };


      worker.onerror = function (event) {
         console.log(event.message, event);
      };


      function sayHello(){
         alert("Hello sir...." );
      }
  </script>
</head>
<body>
   <input type="button" onclick="sayHello();" value="Say Hello"/>
</body>
</html>
```

Checking for Browser Support

Following is the syntax to detect a Web Worker feature support available in a browser:

```
<!DOCTYPE HTML>
<html>
<head>
<title>Big for loop</title>
  <script src="/js/modernizr-1.5.min.js"></script>
  <script>
   if (Modernizr.webworkers) {
      alert("Congratulation!! you have web workers support." );
   }else{
      alert("Sorry!! you do not have web workers support." );
   }
  </script>
</head>
<body>
   <p>Checking for Browser Support for web workers</p>
</body>
```

```
</html>
```

This will produce the following result −

Click me

18.   HTML5 – IndexedDB

The indexeddb is a new HTML5 concept to store the data inside user's browser. indexeddb is more power than local storage and useful for applications that requires to store large amount of the data. These applications can run more efficiency and load faster.

Why to use indexeddb?

The W3C has announced that the Web SQL database is a deprecated local storage specification so web developer should not use this technology any more. indexeddb is an alternative for web SQL data base and more effective than older technologies.

Features

- it stores key-pair values
- it is not a relational database
- IndexedDB API is mostly asynchronous
- it is not a structured query language
- it has supported to access the data from same domain

IndexedDB

Before enter into an indexeddb, we need to add some prefixes of implementation as shown below

```
window.indexedDB = window.indexedDB || window.mozIndexedDB ||
window.webkitIndexedDB || window.msIndexedDB;


window.IDBTransaction = window.IDBTransaction || window.webkitIDBTransaction ||
window.msIDBTransaction;

window.IDBKeyRange = window.IDBKeyRange || window.webkitIDBKeyRange ||
window.msIDBKeyRange


if (!window.indexedDB) {
    window.alert("Your browser doesn't support a stable version of IndexedDB.")
}
```

Open an IndexedDB database

Before creating a database, we have to prepare some data for the data base.let's start with company employee details.

```
const employeeData = [
    { id: "01", name: "Gopal K Varma", age: 35, email:
"zahid@zahidmziwa.com" },
```

```
                  { id: "02", name: "Prasad", age: 24, email: "prasad@zahidmziwa.com" } ];
```

Adding the data

Here adding some data manually into the data as shown below –

```
function add() {
   var request = db.transaction(["employee"], "readwrite")
   .objectStore("employee")
   .add({ id: "01", name: "prasad", age: 24, email: "prasad@zahidmziwa.com     "
});

   request.onsuccess = function(event) {
      alert("Prasad has been added to your database.");
   };

   request.onerror = function(event) {
      alert("Unable to add data\r\nPrasad is already exist in your database! ");
   }
}
```

Retrieving Data

We can retrieve the data from the data base using with get()

```
function read() {
   var transaction = db.transaction(["employee"]);
   var objectStore = transaction.objectStore("employee");
   var request = objectStore.get("00-03");

   request.onerror = function(event) {
      alert("Unable to retrieve daa from database!");
   };

   request.onsuccess = function(event) {
      if(request.result) {
         alert("Name: " + request.result.name + ", Age: " + request.result.age
+ ", Email: " + request.result.email);
      }
```

```
        else {

            alert("Kenny couldn't be found in your database!");

        }

    };

}
```

Using with get(), we can store the data in object instead of that we can store the data in cursor and we can retrieve the data from cursor

```
function readAll() {

    var objectStore = db.transaction("employee").objectStore("employee");


    objectStore.openCursor().onsuccess = function(event) {

        var cursor = event.target.result;


        if (cursor) {

            alert("Name for id " + cursor.key + " is " + cursor.value.name + ",
Age: " + cursor.value.age + ", Email: " + cursor.value.email);

            cursor.continue();

        }


        else {

            alert("No more entries!");

        }

    };

}
```

Removing the data

We can remove the data from IndexedDB with remove().Here is how the code looks like

```
function remove() {

    var request = db.transaction(["employee"], "readwrite")

    .objectStore("employee")

    .delete("02");


    request.onsuccess = function(event) {

        alert("prasad entry has been removed from your database.");

    };

}
```

HTML Code

To show all the data we need to use onClick event as shown below code —

```html
<!DOCTYPE html>
<html>
    <head>

        <meta http-equiv="Content-Type" content="text/html; charset=utf-8" />
        <title>IndexedDb Demo | onlyWebPro.com</title>

    </head>
    <body>

        <button onclick="read()">Read </button>
        <button onclick="readAll()"></button>
        <button onclick="add()"></button>
        <button onclick="remove()">Delete </button>

    </body>
</html>
```

The final code should be as:

```html
<!DOCTYPE html>
<html>
    <head>

        <meta http-equiv="Content-Type" content="text/html; charset=utf-8" />
        <script type="text/javascript">
            //prefixes of implementation that we want to test
            window.indexedDB = window.indexedDB || window.mozIndexedDB ||
window.webkitIndexedDB || window.msIndexedDB;

            //prefixes of window.IDB objects
            window.IDBTransaction = window.IDBTransaction ||
window.webkitIDBTransaction || window.msIDBTransaction;

            window.IDBKeyRange = window.IDBKeyRange || window.webkitIDBKeyRange ||
window.msIDBKeyRange

            if (!window.indexedDB) {
```

```javascript
        window.alert("Your browser doesn't support a stable version of
IndexedDB.")
        }


    const employeeData = [
        { id: "00-01", name: "gopal", age: 35, email:
"zahid@zahidmziwa.com" },
        { id: "00-02", name: "prasad", age: 32, email:
"prasad@zahidmziwa.com" }
    ];
    var db;
    var request = window.indexedDB.open("newDatabase", 1);

    request.onerror = function(event) {
       console.log("error: ");
    };


    request.onsuccess = function(event) {
       db = request.result;
       console.log("success: "+ db);
    };


    request.onupgradeneeded = function(event) {
       var db = event.target.result;
       var objectStore = db.createObjectStore("employee", {keyPath:
"id"});

        for (var i in employeeData) {
           objectStore.add(employeeData[i]);
        }
    }


    function read() {
       var transaction = db.transaction(["employee"]);
       var objectStore = transaction.objectStore("employee");
       var request = objectStore.get("00-03");

        request.onerror = function(event) {
           alert("Unable to retrieve daa from database!");
```

```javascript
            };

            request.onsuccess = function(event) {
                // Do something with the request.result!
                if(request.result) {
                    alert("Name: " + request.result.name + ", Age: " +
request.result.age + ", Email: " + request.result.email);
                }

                else {
                    alert("Kenny couldn't be found in your database!");
                }
            };
        }

        function readAll() {
            var objectStore =
db.transaction("employee").objectStore("employee");

            objectStore.openCursor().onsuccess = function(event) {
                var cursor = event.target.result;

                if (cursor) {
                    alert("Name for id " + cursor.key + " is " +
cursor.value.name + ", Age: " + cursor.value.age + ", Email: " +
cursor.value.email);
                    cursor.continue();
                }

                else {
                    alert("No more entries!");
                }
            };
        }

        function add() {
            var request = db.transaction(["employee"], "readwrite")
            .objectStore("employee")
```

```
            .add({ id: "00-03", name: "Kenny", age: 19, email:
"kenny@planet.org" });

            request.onsuccess = function(event) {
                alert("Kenny has been added to your database.");
            };

            request.onerror = function(event) {
                alert("Unable to add data\r\nKenny is aready exist in your
database! ");
            }
        }

        function remove() {
            var request = db.transaction(["employee"], "readwrite")
            .objectStore("employee")
            .delete("00-03");

            request.onsuccess = function(event) {
                alert("Kenny's entry has been removed from your database.");
            };
        }
    </script>

</head>
<body>

    <button onclick="read()">Read </button>
    <button onclick="readAll()">Read all </button>
    <button onclick="add()">Add data </button>
    <button onclick="remove()">Delete data </button>

</body>
</html>
```

It will produce the following output:

Read | Read all | Add data | Delete data

19.   HTML5 – Web Messaging

Web Messaging is the way for documents to separates browsing context to share the data without Dom. It overrides the cross domain communication problem in different domains, protocols or ports.

For example, you want to send the data from your page to ad container which is placed at iframe or voice-versa, in this scenario, Browser throws a security exception. With web messaging we can pass the data across as a message event.

Message Event

Message events fires Cross-document messaging, channel messaging, server-sent events and web sockets.it has described by Message Event interface.

Attributes

Attributes	Description
data	Contains string data
origin	Contains Domain name and port
lastEventId	Contains unique identifier for the current message event.
source	Contains to A reference to the originating document's window
ports	Contains the data which is sent by any message port

Sending a cross-document message

Before send cross document message, we need to create a new web browsing context either by creating new iframe or new window. We can send the data using with postMessage() and it has two arguments. They are as

- **message** – The message to send
- **targetOrigin** – Origin name

Examples

Sending message from iframe to button

```
var iframe = document.querySelector('iframe');
var button = document.querySelector('button');


var clickHandler = function(){
```

```
    iframe.contentWindow.postMessage('The message to
send.','http://zahidserver.runhosting.net);

}

button.addEventListener('click',clickHandler,false);
```

Receiving a cross-document message in the receiving document

```
var messageEventHandler = function(event){
    // check that the origin is one we want.
    if(event.origin == 'http://zahidserver.runhosting.net'){
        alert(event.data);
    }
}
window.addEventListener('message', messageEventHandler,false);
```

Channel messaging

Two-way communication between the browsing contexts is called channel messaging. It is useful for communication across multiple origins.

The MessageChannel and MessagePort Objects

While creating messageChannel, it internally creates two ports to sending the data and forwarded to another browsing context.

- **postMessage()** – Post the message throw channel
- **start()** – It sends the data
- **close()** – it close the ports

In this scenario, we are sending the data from one iframe to another iframe. Here we are invoking the data in function and passing the data to DOM.

```
var loadHandler = function(){
    var mc, portMessageHandler;
    mc = new MessageChannel();

window.parent.postMessage('documentAHasLoaded','http://foo.example',[mc.port2])
;

    portMessageHandler = function(portMsgEvent){
        alert( portMsgEvent.data );
    }

    mc.port1.addEventListener('message', portMessageHandler, false);
```

```
    mc.port1.start();
}
window.addEventListener('DOMContentLoaded', loadHandler, false);
```

Above code, it is taking the data from port 2, now it will pass the data to second iframe

```
var loadHandler = function(){
    var iframes, messageHandler;

    iframes = window.frames;
    messageHandler = function(messageEvent){
        if( messageEvent.ports.length > 0 ){
            // transfer the port to iframe[1]

iframes[1].postMessage('portopen','http://foo.example',messageEvent.ports);
        }
    }
    window.addEventListener('message',messageHandler,false);
}
window.addEventListener('DOMContentLoaded',loadHandler,false);
```

Now second document handles the data by using the portMsgHandler function.

```
var loadHandler(){
    // Define our message handler function
    var messageHandler = function(messageEvent){

        // Our form submission handler
        var formHandler = function(){
            var msg = 'add <foo@example.com> to game circle.';
            messageEvent.ports[0].postMessage(msg);
        }
        document.forms[0].addEventListener('submit',formHandler,false);
    }
    window.addEventListener('message',messageHandler,false);
}
window.addEventListener('DOMContentLoaded',loadHandler,false);
```

Cross-origin resource sharing (CORS) is a mechanism to allows the restricted resources from another domain in web browser

For suppose, if you click on *HTML5- video player* in html5 demo sections. it will ask camera permission. if user allow the permission then only it will open the camera or else it doesn't open the camera for web applications

Making a CORS request

here Chrome, Firefox, Opera and Safari all use the XMLHttprequest2 object and Internet Explorer uses the similar XDomainRequest object, object.

```
function createCORSRequest(method, url) {

   var xhr = new XMLHttpRequest();


   if ("withCredentials" in xhr) {

      // Check if the XMLHttpRequest object has a "withCredentials" property.

      // "withCredentials" only exists on XMLHTTPRequest2 objects.

      xhr.open(method, url, true);

   }
   else if (typeof XDomainRequest != "undefined") {

      // Otherwise, check if XDomainRequest.

      // XDomainRequest only exists in IE, and is IE's way of making CORS
requests.

      xhr = new XDomainRequest();

      xhr.open(method, url);

   }


   else {

      // Otherwise, CORS is not supported by the browser.

      xhr = null;

   }

   return xhr;

}
var xhr = createCORSRequest('GET', url);

if (!xhr) {

   throw new Error('CORS not supported');

}
```

Event handles in CORS

Event Handler	Description
onloadstart	Starts the request
onprogress	Loads the data and send the data
onabort	Abort the request
onerror	request has failed
onload	request load successfully
ontimeout	time out has happened before request could complete
onloadend	When the request is complete either successful or failure

Example of onload or onerror event

```
xhr.onload = function() {
    var responseText = xhr.responseText;

    // process the response.
    console.log(responseText);
};

xhr.onerror = function() {
    console.log('There was an error!');
};
```

Example of CORS with handler

Below example will show the example of makeCorsRequest() and onload handler

```
// Create the XHR object.
function createCORSRequest(method, url) {
    var xhr = new XMLHttpRequest();

    if ("withCredentials" in xhr) {

        // XHR for Chrome/Firefox/Opera/Safari.
        xhr.open(method, url, true);
```

```javascript
    }

    else if (typeof XDomainRequest != "undefined") {
        // XDomainRequest for IE.
        xhr = new XDomainRequest();
        xhr.open(method, url);
    }

    else {
        // CORS not supported.
        xhr = null;
    }
    return xhr;
}

// Helper method to parse the title tag from the response.
function getTitle(text) {
    return text.match('<title>(.*)?</title>')[1];
}

// Make the actual CORS request.
function makeCorsRequest() {

    // All HTML5 Rocks properties support CORS.
    var url = 'http://zahidserver.runhosting.net';

    var xhr = createCORSRequest('GET', url);

    if (!xhr) {
        alert('CORS not supported');
        return;
    }

    // Response handlers.
    xhr.onload = function() {
        var text = xhr.responseText;
        var title = getTitle(text);
        alert('Response from CORS request to ' + url + ': ' + title);
```

```
    };

    xhr.onerror = function() {
        alert('Woops, there was an error making the request.');
    };
    xhr.send();
}
```

Web RTC introduced by World Wide Web Consortium (W3C). That supports browser-to-browser applications for voice calling, video chat, and P2P file sharing.

If you want to try out? web RTC available for Chrome, Opera, and Firefox. A good place to start is the simple video chat application at Web RTC implements three API's as shown below –

- **MediaStream** – get access to the user's camera and microphone.
- **RTCPeerConnection** – get access to audio or video calling facility.
- **RTCDataChannel** – get access to peer-to-peer communication.

MediaStream

The MediaStream represents synchronized streams of media, For an example, Click on HTML5 Video player in HTML5 demo section or else visit
https://simpl.info/getusermedia/

The above example contains stream.getAudioTracks() and stream.VideoTracks(). If there is no audio tracks, it returns an empty array and it will check video stream,if webcam connected, stream.getVideoTracks() returns an array of one MediaStreamTrack representing the stream from the webcam. A simple example is chat applications, a chat application gets stream from web camera, rear camera, microphone.

Sample code of MediaStream

```
function gotStream(stream) {

    window.AudioContext = window.AudioContext || window.webkitAudioContext;

    var audioContext = new AudioContext();


    // Create an AudioNode from the stream

    var mediaStreamSource = audioContext.createMediaStreamSource(stream);


    // Connect it to destination to hear yourself

    // or any other node for processing!

    mediaStreamSource.connect(audioContext.destination);

}

navigator.getUserMedia({audio:true}, gotStream);
```

Screen capture

It's also possible in Chrome browser with mediaStreamSource and it requires HTTPS. This feature is not yet available in opera.

Session Control, Network & Media Information

Web RTC required peer-to-peer communication between browsers. This mechanism required signaling, network information, session control and media information. Web developers can choose different mechanism to communicate between the browsers such as SIP or XMPP or any two way communications.

Sample code of createSignalingChannel()

```
var signalingChannel = createSignalingChannel();
var pc;
var configuration = ...;

// run start(true) to initiate a call
function start(isCaller) {
    pc = new RTCPeerConnection(configuration);

    // send any ice candidates to the other peer
    pc.onicecandidate = function (evt) {
        signalingChannel.send(JSON.stringify({ "candidate": evt.candidate }));
    };

    // once remote stream arrives, show it in the remote video element
    pc.onaddstream = function (evt) {
        remoteView.src = URL.createObjectURL(evt.stream);
    };

    // get the local stream, show it in the local video element and send it
    navigator.getUserMedia({ "audio": true, "video": true }, function (stream) {
        selfView.src = URL.createObjectURL(stream);
        pc.addStream(stream);

        if (isCaller)
            pc.createOffer(gotDescription);

        else
            pc.createAnswer(pc.remoteDescription, gotDescription);

            function gotDescription(desc) {
                pc.setLocalDescription(desc);
                signalingChannel.send(JSON.stringify({ "sdp": desc }));
```

```
            }
        });
    }

    signalingChannel.onmessage = function (evt) {
        if (!pc)
            start(false);
            var signal = JSON.parse(evt.data);

        if (signal.sdp)
            pc.setRemoteDescription(new RTCSessionDescription(signal.sdp));

        else
            pc.addIceCandidate(new RTCIceCandidate(signal.candidate));
    };
```

Printed in Great Britain
by Amazon

78391360R00096